I Made Them
for Hope

Revelations of God in Everyday Life

Carolyn Wing Greenlee

"I Made Them for Hope"
Revelations of God in Everyday Life

Editor: Dan Worley
Layout and cover: Dan Worley
Cover photo by Carolyn Wing Greenlee

ISBN
978-1-887400-80-0 (paperback)
978-1-887400-81-7 (kindle)

Earthen Vessel Productions
www.earthen.com

Contents

Part 1

Help with Little Things

I call them *Minuscule Miracles* because the accounts in this book are mostly small, though some are more than that. All of them come from my own experiences or from friends and family close to me. I did know a man who prayed for a little boy who had been blinded when a battery exploded in his face, and that little boy received brand-new eyeballs—but none of these stories are on that scale.

For me, these little divine interventions are significant and worth writing down because they show how much God cares about us. Just think—the One who created the heavens, the earth, and everything in them still hears—and cares—about the mundane, the unspectacular, the seemingly insignificant. But I find this truly monumental because it's so personal, so detailed, so caring. And so surprising. They're surprising because we know He's magnificent and mighty, but we don't always realize how tender, gentle, thoughtful, and personal He is.

My neighbor Moe surprised me one day when she said, "I asked God to help me thread my sewing needle, and He did."

Really? The God of the universe threads Moe's needles?

Yes. Still does. She told me, "He threads it, and then I put more than enough thread in it so we don't have to do it again. I know He's a busy Guy."

Well, I had to try it. So I asked. And you know what? He did it! Just to make sure it wasn't a fluke, I tried several times, and each time my needle was threaded.

Of course, I had to share it. I mentioned it to some ladies at church. A few Sundays later, several of them were smiling broadly at me and mimicking the act of threading a needle. They were thrilled. Me too!

Moe also told me that God helps her put on her earrings. So

I tried that, too. You'd think it wouldn't be that difficult, but sometimes the backing is tiny, and you have to line it up with the little post on the decorative part. It's easy to drop, and then there's the maddening hunt for the missing piece. But ever since Moe told me God helps her with her earrings, I've been asking Him as well—and it's wonderful because He helps me every time.

That's how I discovered that God will even help with the smallest things, like working the clasp on a necklace. It's not a big deal compared to world events or terrible illnesses, but when your fingers don't work as well as they used to, even simple tasks can be frustrating. When things that were once easy become difficult, it can make you feel inept—even helpless, hopeless, and old.

But when the Lord of All hears me and the clasp closes securely on the ring, I feel a surge of gratitude and amazement that He would do such a thing for me. And suddenly, I don't feel helpless anymore.

How can I feel helpless when God Himself is my Helper?

Carol's Earrings

My dear friend Carol had a pair of earrings that her daughter, Stephanie, had given her. They were silver and dangly, with a blue stone. She loved them and wore them often.

One day, after returning home from a walk with her dogs, Angel and Fritz, she noticed one of the earrings was missing. Immediately, she retraced her steps, scanning the ground for any sign of it, but found nothing. Mystified, she searched her house—checking under furniture and cushions—but it was nowhere to be found.

About three weeks later, Carol was sitting on her couch, talking on the phone with a friend from church. One of the dogs' stuffed animals lay a few feet away on the floor near the sliding glass door. "The dogs and I walk through that area a couple of times a day," she said. "That toy hadn't been there before, but they do carry them around, so it wasn't surprising to see it there." But then she noticed something else. "I saw something shiny between its front legs. I went over and looked more closely. It was the earring! How could this be? The carpet had been vacuumed three times since I lost it!"

"I screamed to my friend on the phone, 'My earring! I just found my earring!' My friend and I celebrated and praised the Lord. I couldn't believe it—after three weeks, it had turned up right in my house!

"It was such a miracle. It helped me realize how much the Lord cares for us and wants to bless us—even when it comes to something small like an earring, of no real value except that my daughter gave them to me, and I loved them and wore them all the time."

Not long ago, Carol lost another earring, a gold hoop that attached to itself, with six little beads—red, white, and silver—loose on the hoop. Apparently, she hadn't fastened it properly, and it must have fallen off during one of her dog walks around the complex where she lived.

A few days later, there was a Homeowners Association meeting at the clubhouse. Carol said, "Usually, when I come out of my gate, I turn right, walk half a block up my street, and cross the parking lot on the right to the clubhouse. But that day, I turned left, planning to cross the lawn and go around the back of my house to the sidewalk in front of the marina. From there, it's a straight path to the clubhouse."

Carol was walking along the upper edge of her lawn toward the sidewalk, and when she was about halfway across, she spotted something shiny in the grass. It was her earring! Gleefully, she retrieved it and went on to the meeting. Then she noticed one of the red beads was missing.

After the meeting, she returned to where she had found the earring. With the thick grass standing about three inches high, how could she ever find a tiny red bead? Then she heard the Lord say, "Rake it."

Carol had only a mini rake—a rectangle of red plastic about six inches wide attached to a short wooden handle. She told me, "Years before, my husband, Randy, had given me the little red rake as a gift—supposedly so I could help with the yard work and rake leaves, etc. It was kind of a joke, but I kept it and have always used and enjoyed it."

Carol immediately fetched the mini rake and returned to the spot where she had found her missing earring. Once again, she stood looking at the grassy expanse. Where, in all that green, was the bead?

"It was such a God moment," she said. "On the very first pass I made with that mini rake, the bead popped up and landed right on top of the grass."

I love this story. The God who spoke hundreds of billions of stars into beautifully colored configurations—the God who created everything and keeps it all in place with the word of His power—cares enough about one small human child to lead her to the very spot where a tiny red bead lay hidden in the grass. And I bet her amazement, thankfulness, and exuberant joy made Him smile.

Nathan and the Horses

As an experienced photographer with a unique and intriguing aesthetic, my friend Nathan has many opportunities to travel the world, capturing images in unusual places he is privileged to visit. I must admit I was thoroughly envious when he said he was in Argentina staying at a ranch that was known for its superb horses.

He told me there were many picturesque scenes, but he always looks beyond the usual. He found it in a wide expanse of flat grassland—a pasture for the horses. In the far background was a line of trees, and standing in front of him was a single, dramatic tree. Against the pale backdrop of land and sky, it stood out—stunning, stark, compelling. Nathan said, "It had a nice shape, with no leaves—a picturesque tree. Everything was set up for this to be a good scene, something I was looking for that would be a little different, but it needed some horses." But there were none in sight. Quietly, he said, "It would be great if some horses were in it."

It was a heart-whispered prayer—nothing fancy, forceful, or fervent—yet God heard him.

"I didn't see them coming," Nathan said, "but there were six horses that came walking up in a line and literally stood in front of that tree, perfectly arranged."

You might think it was simply serendipity. He was standing there, and the horses were on their way to one of their favorite spots in the pasture. But he said, "The horses were out of sight— and then they just showed up."

Or maybe Nathan simply has a way with animals, and indeed, they seem drawn to his gentle nature—he tells me he connects well with his cat. But to my knowledge, nothing like this had ever happened to him before—or since.

When I asked him how it affected him, Nathan said, "It felt playful. It was very unexpected. It felt like prayer was heard and then I could just enjoy it."

God creates each human being as an original, designed for the time and setting into which He would place that precious child on Earth. Each one is unique, and with each one He can have a unique relationship. He speaks with us in language we can understand, tailored to our own perceptions and personality.

Over the years, God has revealed Himself to me in many ways, but I can certainly say "playful" hasn't been one of them. But He is infinite, multi-faceted, so vast and limitless, with endless revelation of depth and height and length and breadth of goodness and love, that no one person can know it all. But when we hear each other's stories, we get to add their understandings to ours.

Playful. I never would have thought of that word. But I can see it now through Nathan's eyes. There were the horses, walking up in an obedient line, then positioning themselves precisely in

the most picturesque way. Playful. A moment of pure delight—
something to simply sit back and enjoy.

The Cloud

My friend Debra and her partner were heading to a family
reunion in Moab, Utah, with her grandma in the back seat. They
were driving through the desert in Debra's new car, which did
not have air conditioning.

Debra said, "I kept checking on her—'You doing okay back
there, Grandma?' She just smiled. Then I noticed she had shade
in the back seat. I thought that was odd. It didn't make sense.
Then I saw a little cloud following us. I think she must have
prayed.

"All across the desert, Grandma had shade in the back seat.
The cloud kept her nice and comfortable the whole way."

I love that the little cloud followed them all the way to
their journey's end. It also reminds me of another cloud that
moved along with travelers—the pillar of cloud that guided the
children of Israel through the wilderness, shading them from the
blistering heat of the desert.

When Debra first told me this story, I thought it was charming
and sweet, a beautiful reminder of God's care for a little old lady.
It truly is all of that. But it also brings to mind one of the songs
in the Bible that says the Lord is our Keeper, and the sun shall
not smite us by day.

When I think God is much too big, mighty, and busy to be
bothered with tiny matters, I realize I make Him too small. I'm
not saying He's like a celestial butler, here to keep us comfortable
in all circumstances and adversities. Rather, I believe He's more
gracious than we realize and more caring than we can imagine.

John's Healing

When my son John was a teenager, he came down with
a mysterious illness that caused such high fevers and severe
headaches that he couldn't bear light and was too sick to get out

of bed. My husband and I did all we could for him, but nothing helped. He was miserable for days.

Then one morning, I heard my son's voice saying cheerily, "I'm well, Mom." His eyes were bright, and he was smiling. Astonished, I askcd what had happened.

He said he had been lying there, suffering from the terrible pain in his head, when he prayed, "Lord, the leper came and said, 'If You are willing, You can heal me.' Jesus, if You are willing, please heal me."

John said he heard a voice say, "I am willing." At that moment, he saw something like a sticker on his forehead. It peeled away, and instantly, the headache and fever were gone.

That was forty years ago, and yet, whenever I read the account of Jesus and the leper, I always think of my son John. Scripture says the leper came to Jesus, and Jesus, moved with compassion, said, "I am willing. Be cleansed."

I love that the Lord of lords and King of kings heard the voice of a teenager in pain, alone in the dark, was moved with compassion, and healed him. And He is still moved with compassion. And He is still willing.

A Leaky Ceiling

My friend Carol and I were about to leave on a little mini vacation. Just before we went out the door, she noticed a puddle of water on her entryway floor. Looking up, she saw a huge bulge in the paint on the ceiling. Because she had a repair policy, she was able to quickly make arrangements to get the leak fixed, but she was annoyed about the mess. I told her it was a blessing that she had seen it before we left. It would have been much, much worse to find it after she got back.

In this life, rain will fall and leaks may come, but the Lord had kept this one from being worse, and when Carol saw that truth, she rejoiced, and we went on our way feeling blessed.

It's so easy to be annoyed at the inconvenience and not realize what is really going on. It reminds me of the time I was complaining to God, saying, "Why didn't You protect me?"

He said quietly, "I protected you more than you know."

The Letter

Recently we had several days of furious rain. Streets in Lakeport looked like lakes. Friends reported leaks in their ceilings. I kept an eye—and an ear—out.

Last winter, there were some pretty alarming leaks, with water streaming from the ceiling near my dining room table, just a yard or two from my computer. Dan had gone up on the roof and done his best to fix it. So far this year, no leaks—but I had buckets at the ready, just in case.

On the fourth night of rain, I couldn't sleep. I needed to write a letter to encourage a friend struggling with despair and hopelessness, but I had been putting it off, unsure of what to say. But that night, I had such a sense of urgency. I felt compelled to go upstairs. I figured God wanted me to write that letter, so I sat down at my computer and asked Him to give me the words my friend needed.

I had just begun to type when I heard the sound of dripping. I paused and listened. Yep. Definitely water dripping. I could hear it hitting the carpet. I grabbed a bucket and placed it beneath the wet spot on the rug.

Perhaps "miracle" is too strong a word for what happened. "Blessing" is probably more fitting. The Lord got me upstairs just in time to catch the drips before they did much damage, and He gave me the words my friend needed—so she would know she was loved and that neither the Lord nor I had forgotten her.

Lost Wallets

My friend Dan had gone to the supermarket, and as he got out of his car, he saw a young woman about to return her shopping cart to the store. Since he needed a cart anyway, he told her he would take it in for her. She thanked him and then drove away.

It wasn't until he was inside the store and had placed the first item in the cart that he noticed her wallet sitting in the child's seat. Hoping she would realize it was missing and come back for it, he went outside and waited. She didn't return. Not feeling comfortable going through the woman's wallet to find out who she was or how to contact her, he decided to trust it to the lady at Customer Service. She assured him it would be kept in the safe and returned to the customer.

Dan told me he has never kept a wallet he's found—not only because he was raised that way but because of something that happened to him when he was a young man driving a taxi.

One night, at the end of his shift, he went back to the garage to turn in his fares when he realized his wallet was missing. It contained all his fares and tips. With a shock, he remembered leaving it on the roof of his taxi while giving change to his last customer. Not only had he lost his tips and his share of the fares, he was also responsible for the company's share, and would have to work for free until it was repaid. It was a significant loss, and he was devastated.

Dan drove back to the area where he thought he'd lost it, but the wallet was nowhere to be found. Later that day, he received a call from a man who said he'd found the wallet in the middle of the road.

Gratefully, Dan met the man, who handed him the wallet. All the money was still inside. When Dan tried to give the man a reward, he refused, saying, "Maybe someone will do the same for me someday, and maybe you'll do the same for others."

And ever since, that's exactly what Dan has done.

We affect each other. That man may never know what his honesty and kindness did for Dan, but God knows, and He has His own unique ways of blessing those who choose to do good for others instead of thinking only of themselves.

Katerina's Bible

I wanted to give Katerina a Bible, but she was leaving for Prague in three days. No time to order one. I used to have a lot of them in different versions, but I had given most of them away. So I prayed about it and felt nudged to give her mine. It wasn't a big sacrifice. I really wanted to do it. It's very special to receive your first Bible from someone who loves you. The New King James Bible was beautiful with a sleek black cover and shiny gold edges and the text was in a font that was friendly and easy to read.

The night before Katerina came for one last visit, I told Dan I was giving her my Bible. I said I'd get another New King James later. I planned to look for a study Bible with footnotes and reference materials.

Dan said, "I just found one of your old Bibles down at the studio." He was pretty sure it was a New King James and went and got it. I didn't remember that it was an Open Bible, a version designed for serious study of the Scriptures, but inside I had written my name and the date, June 2. There was no year, but from the notes I had written in the margins, I figure it must have been around thirty-eight years ago, which explained why I didn't remember it.

I was flabbergasted as I looked through the pages. It had everything I wanted and more. And it showed up right after I decided to give my own away.

I hoped Katerina would feel loved when she received the Bible from me that day. She had one in Czech from when she was doing studies in comparative religions, but then she was an atheist brought up under Communism and reading the holy books of all the world's religions. When she read the Bible, it was just another collection of writings by human beings, not a treasury of truth and the revelation of God Himself to a newborn child of the King. I thought my own Bible in English would give her a fresh way of reading about her Savior and it would be a precious gift from my hands to hers.

Then there she was, my dear, sweet friend. I told her I had a present for her and held the Bible out to her. She said she couldn't accept such a personal gift, but I told her about the wonderful Open Bible that Dan just happened to find.

So she took the Bible and began carefully turning the pages. Abruptly she stopped, surprised. Some of the words had caught her eye because they were red.

I explained they were the words of Jesus and they were printed in red to make everything He said easy to find, and also to remind us of His blood, the payment for our sins. A bit shaken, Katerina read the words to me—"Do not be afraid… I am with you. …I have many people in this city." Astonished, she said it was exactly what she needed. She was returning to Prague where she felt so alone and the first words she read in her new Bible seemed to have been written specifically for her.

I explained that she had just received a *rhema* word from God. That's when words from the Bible leap off the page and go straight into your heart. It was a divine gift to her from Jesus. I told her the Bible is not a collection of rules, myths, and moral tales, it's a living, God-breathed book and God Himself would speak to her through it often and in different ways.

I thought it was so tenderly personal that Jesus would give His new child a *rhema* word—that the first thing that happened when she opened the book was a reassurance that He knew her worries and would be with her in the city in which she felt so alone. I told her to read her Bible every day, and every day God would speak to her exactly what she needed to hear.

When I was a Taoist, I thought I had to go it alone, stumbling along by trial and error trying to keep from getting crosswise with the Tao—the impersonal force that simply is. But Christianity isn't a religious system with a path we must try to discern and decode until we reach the end of the road, at which time we will find out whether we qualify for whatever reward awaits those who are worthy. It's a change of nature, the start of a supernatural life (above-natural) which includes the privilege of walking and talking with the Father of Eternities every day.

For dear Katerina, now taking her first steps in her brand-new life, Jesus has reassured her she won't ever have to go it alone.

And at the end of the journey, she won't have to wonder if she's "made it." She has already been accepted by God and her last step on Earth will be her first step into her Forever Eternal Home.

The Artist's Heart

I enjoy talking to creative people, especially when they're willing to tell me what's behind the painting, the lyrics to the song, the characters of their story. And I think the artist enjoys it too. My artist friend Bill Anderson says, "When someone likes my artwork, it makes me feel like time and effort to be creative is worthwhile. I am pleased when my artwork is valued and respected and I hope it makes an impact on the individual."

You can learn a lot about people by the things they say about what they've made. I found that out one day when I decided to take a closer look at the weeds around my house. Vetch is ubiquitous where I live. It's a nuisance—a fast-growing, troublesome weed, difficult to eradicate and quick to overtake a garden. But that day, I decided to take the time to examine more closely the flowers that were plentiful in the tangled mass of leaves.

They turned out to be little purple trumpets lined up on stems—their delicate petals shading from light to dark with golden stamens deep inside. I told God, "It was so nice of You to put such pretty flowers on the weeds. You could have made everything gray."

"I'm so glad you noticed," He replied. "I made them for hope."

Really? I was startled. The Lord of the Universe had just told me He designed colors and beauty specifically to give hope to us human beings. But then He went on.

"Have you ever noticed that the first thing out of bare branches after winter is not leaves but blossoms?" Instantly, I had a vision of slender branches laden with pure white blossoms, their petals fluttering in the sunlight. Then I saw puppies, kittens, fluffy little yellow chicks—all of them adorable baby animals.

Then I saw an old man standing on a broken-down wooden

porch, his face under the torn brim of his hat, grizzled, unshaven, and deeply lined with hard times. His clothes were shabby, his shoes were worn out, and so was he. Nearby, a little kitten batted at a bit of fluff floating in a patch of sunlight. As the old man watched the kitten, I saw the faintest of smiles cross his face. In my heart, I understood that God had intentionally created things that can reach past the sorrows, if only for a moment.

Bill says every piece of artwork has a story. There's a message in it, something he wants to say, and if I ask him, he is pleased to tell me more.

It's been more than thirty years, but I can still see the vetch and the vision of the blossoms, the baby animals, the kitten, and the old man. I can still hear God's voice, sharing His intention when He created those things—handiwork that He intended to be a clear message of His heart towards us. As Bill said about his own artwork, he wanted it to have an impact on the viewer. The Bible has many passages about God's creation—its glory, its magnificence, its power and beauty—but it wasn't until I paused and admired the little purple flowers on the troublesome weed that He revealed to me something so tender and thoughtful that I never would have otherwise known.

God wants us to know Him. We have glimpses of His majesty and creative genius in mountains and the intricate designs on a butterfly's wings, but we can't know His heart unless He tells us.

Now here's the amazing thing: He wants us to know Him. Really? The Creator of the universe? Infinite, omnipotent, omniscient, omnipresent, unsearchable, holy God? We can know Him? Well, at least a little. And we can know more and more if we really want to.

How? Through His Word. He has revealed His nature in what He says about Himself and how He interacts with humanity through history. The Bible is an accurate record of thousands of years of His works and ways.

It's an ancient book written by sixty-six authors over a couple of thousand years. You can study it, seeing the accuracy of historical events verified in the archaeological diggings in the Holy Land, corroborated in the writings of secular historians such as Joséphus and Herodotus, and in eyewitness accounts of those who knew Him in His incarnation, further verified by the more than 300 prophecies Jesus fulfilled in His life on Earth. But you can learn all those things and still not know Him. Here's the most supernatural part of the Christian life: You can know Him personally.

How is that possible? The same way you cultivate any relationship. You talk. You spend time together. Here's an example:

Byron Carniglia was the Department of Forestry's Fire Chief of Napa County, California, for thirty years. Many people knew his name. He had a reputation for sound leadership, good judgment, fairness, integrity, competence, and wisdom. They had heard about his actions in past fire seasons and admired his excellent decisions resulting in efficient strategies and deployment of firefighters and equipment. They knew a lot about him, but they didn't necessarily know him. He was in charge of probably several hundred people, all of whom knew his name, but I'm sure some never met him and perhaps some had never even seen him.

They wouldn't necessarily know he could play the piano really well, but I did. Byron was Dan's uncle and we recorded an album of him playing his favorite songs.

Dan and I spent time with Byron. We went to his house and visited with him and his wife Nancy and their kids, Pamela and Anthony. Nancy's homemade rolls are legendary, and she and I have shared some significant prayer times together. Pamela is a reader, a literary lady who likes my books, so of course we have a lot to talk about. Dan thought Anthony was such a terrific young man that he wanted our friend Stephanie to marry him. We enjoyed each other. We spent time together.

One lovely afternoon, Byron was standing on my back deck looking at the lake with Dan and me. Byron said, "That bay tree in your yard needs to come down. In a fire, it will go up like a torch."

I loved that bay tree. It was shapely and deeply green. I had no idea it was such a hazard, but I understood immediately that its fragrant leaves were full of oil, which is why they were so flammable. So, the tree came down.

I knew Byron Carniglia personally. I spent time with him. And I had a solemn regard for him. I trusted his knowledge and experience, and when he said the bay tree was a danger to me and my property, I believed him and took appropriate action.

Byron wasn't there at my house to look for things to cut down. He was there visiting, enjoying the view. But because he was by profession always aware of what was all around him, he let me know that there was a potential problem and told me what to do about it.

It's that way with God. When you invite Him into your life, you have His invitation to know Him on a personal basis. And when He sees what can hurt you and points it out, you know it's not because He's trying to boss you around or take away things you love; it's because there's a danger you didn't know about and He wants you to be safe.

I think many people believe God exists, and may even have some awe of Him, but they don't know He loves them personally. They don't know how deep and rich and adventurous life becomes when they walk and talk with Him every day as Friend to friend. And they probably don't know He made baby animals especially adorable on purpose to encourage human beings, but I do, because one day I was admiring His handiwork and He said, "I'm so glad you noticed. I made them for hope."

Kathy and the Whales

For 28 years, my friend Kathy has been going to Baja, California, to see the migration of Gray whales. She goes out with a group of others in a little boat, floating in a lagoon among the huge, gentle creatures. Whether Kathy is gifted as an animal communicator or the whales simply feel her love and admiration, she always has remarkable times with them. This last trip, a mama whale brought her calf over for Kathy to admire, and my friend had the thrill of caressing the tongue of a baby whale.

I include this account, not as a miracle, but as a blessing—a faint, wistful glimpse into what God intended originally in the Garden of Eden when all He made was still good and unsullied. There was peace among all creatures, and nobody ate anybody else.

When Kathy looks into the eye of a magnificent whale—so trusting, so calm, so close—she sees intelligence and understanding that one can only gain from years in deep places where others cannot go. And for a moment, that knowing passes between them, heart to heart, in the communion that our Creator always intended us to share.

Part 2

Lunch for Stephanie

Before I moved my computer to my home office so I could do my work without as many distractions, I worked with my young friend Stephanie in the office, which was part of the studio next door.

One morning, when I was preparing my lunch, I realized I had much more than I could possibly eat. *Well*, I thought, *perhaps I can share it with Stephanie.*

When Stephanie arrived, I told her I had made more food than I needed and invited her to help me eat it. She smiled and said she had been on her way to the office when she realized she'd forgotten to make lunch for herself. She was wondering what she was going to do when she heard God say, "Don't worry. Carolyn will have something for you."

It's been more than twenty years since Stephanie worked at Earthen Vessel, but that story sticks in my mind because God told her, *"Carolyn will have something for you."* He used my name. I know He mentions quite a few specific names in the Bible—prophets, priests, kings, nations, rivers, mountains, cities, streets, and more—but that's ancient information embedded in pages written thousands of years ago. Here, in the present days of my little, rather anonymous life, He spoke my name to my friend and also caused me to make more food than I needed so I could provide lunch for Stephanie, whose name and needs He also knew very well.

Nudges

Stephanie and I began visiting Bea Cull when she was in her eighties. She had loved and served Jesus all her life, and we wanted to spend time with this wonderful woman of God, asking her questions and hearing her surprising answers. She wasn't like anyone we had ever met, and every visit was a treat.

Bea and her husband had planted churches in remote areas around the country, living without electricity or the amenities of modern life far into the western wilds. Laughing, she told us she didn't get any credit for that because she liked to camp.

They were living miles from town and serving without wages, but God always supplied what they needed. Once, they had run out of kerosene, and that very day, two friends showed up with more. They had traveled many days by ferry and small dirt roads to reach them just as the kerosene ran out. Bea said God would have had to nudge them to make that trip two weeks earlier in order for the timing to be so perfect.

Another time, she told us she had begun craving the taste of ketchup. They had no money, and there were no stores nearby. But a knock came on the door, and there stood a friend with a paper bag full of groceries—sticking out right on top was a bottle of ketchup.

I sighed and said I had always wished I could have that kind of experience, but I supposed you had to be out in the boonies, in ministry, and in great need in order to see that level of miraculous provision.

Bea said, "Oh no! God is doing that sort of thing for you all the time. You don't need ketchup, but haven't you ever had a friend call just when you needed it? It's the same thing. He knows our needs and often provides for them through the loving touch of a thoughtful friend."

Surprised, I realized, *Oh yes! That had happened many times.* My phone would ring, and I'd hear Stephanie's voice saying, "You've been on my heart, so I thought I'd call and see how you're doing."

My friend Debra does the same thing, only she calls it "ESPN" and tells me the Lord has been pinging her and won't leave her alone. "I don't know what it's about," she'll say, "but you're supposed to talk and I'm supposed to listen." It's always something, and it's always just what I need right then.

If Bea hadn't pointed out the care of God for us in providing the concern of a friend (much more needed than a bottle of ketchup), I don't know that I would have recognized this loving act as God's watchful provision.

It's supernatural, that divine nudging. Debra felt it for the first time many years ago when she was just coming back to the Lord after years of living apart from Him. She was in a rather devastated state, having left all she had behind, including financial security. At the same time, her sister had also just left a toxic marriage and was living in her own devastated state with two young boys and no financial support. When they left their former lives, both of these sisters stepped deeply into poverty. In her freezer, Debra had just one pound of frozen hamburger.

One day, Debra got a persistent thought. She wasn't sure what it was, but it wouldn't leave her alone. All through the morning, she kept feeling that she should take the package of hamburger to her sister.

"I wasn't used to listening to the voice of the Lord in my spirit at that point," Debra said, "and I thought, *This is really strange, but okay.*

"So I grabbed the package of hamburger and drove to my sister's, knocked on her front door, and said, 'I don't understand this, and you're probably going to think it's really weird, but all morning I've been getting the thought that I need to bring this hamburger to you. It's like this thought just won't leave. I don't understand it, but here I am with one pound of hamburger I had to bring to you because I'm supposed to for reasons that I don't understand.'"

"My sister was so happy. She said, 'Oh my gosh, Deb! I've been praying. I've been fixing food for my boys and keep telling the Lord, *I just want to fix them something with hamburger in it—not a lot, just some hamburger for my two little boys.*'

"She told me, 'I've been talking to God about it. I think it would be a really big thing for me and for them to be able to give them something they so much want.'"

Debra told me, "That was one of my first experiences of listening to the voice of the Lord and being obedient to it without really knowing what it was or how it worked."

I told Debra I liked how precise it was. She said, "It was very precise and very direct and very persistent. My sister had been back to the Lord much longer than I had. She was a huge part of my coming back to Him. I had been praying about it and running as hard as I could in the opposite direction."

When God sends one pound of hamburger, or a bottle of ketchup, we can see a certain sweet thoughtfulness in His provision beyond the actual need. But I also saw something gracious in what God did for Debra when He wouldn't leave her alone—a way of letting her know He had welcomed her back. Furthermore, He wanted her to know without a doubt that He had purposes for her life and that He had designed her with supernatural spiritual gifts she didn't even know she had.

It's always so uplifting when you realize you have heard the Lord, and—crazy as it seems—when you obey, wonderful things happen. And then there are times when you don't see wonders and realize you may never know why He told you to do what He told you to do.

Such was the case when Stephanie was having trouble with her neighbor but didn't know why. She had even gone to see her and apologized in case she had offended her in some way, but no offense was stated, so Stephanie remained mystified.

This sweet young lady makes a point of doing her best not only to get along with everyone but also to be a blessing to them. So she continued to be as cordial and friendly to the neighbor as she could, but nothing she did or said made any difference. The neighbor simply made it clear that she couldn't stand her. So Stephanie earnestly sought the Lord, and He told her to make the neighbor a chocolate cream pie.

Did Stephanie go to Safeway and buy a frozen chocolate cream pie? Of course not. She went out and bought the best ingredients she could find and made a scrumptious dessert from scratch.

Carefully, Stephanie took it to the neighbor's house, but the neighbor was not there. When her daughter opened the door, Stephanie held out the freshly made pie. The woman took it and exclaimed, "Oh, that's her favorite!"

I asked Stephanie if she noticed any changes in her neighbor's attitude toward her after that, and she said there was perhaps a tiny bit less animosity, but nothing significant.

God doesn't tell us what will happen when we obey; He just tells us what we should do. We may never know what our obedience brought about, if anything. But what touches me about this story is that God knew the neighbor's favorite dessert was chocolate cream pie—and that's what He told Stephanie to make for her.

By the way, Stephanie told me she made another chocolate cream pie for her own family, but even though she followed the same directions and used the same excellent ingredients, it wasn't as good. Apparently, God had given a special blessing to that original pie.

José

One late afternoon, Dan noticed a dark spot on the ceiling of my home office. "Is that a spider?" he asked. He went closer and reached up. It didn't move. He touched the sheetrock nearby. It was a little soft and moist. When he looked closer, he saw it was not a spider. It was black mold.

Dan knew exactly who to call and was really happy to hear that José "just happened" to be finishing a job about forty-five minutes away. And though it was getting late, he said he would be right over as soon as he was done.

José is one of those handymen who is conscientious, competent, quick, reliable, reasonable, and a joy to have around. He is known for being able to solve complex and bewildering problems. He told me there have been many times when he has been confronted with situations he has never seen before, but he always prays and asks God to help him figure it out—and He always does.

It didn't take José long to replace the leaking pipe in the ceiling of my office and button it all back up so neatly that we couldn't even tell where the repair was made.

Meanwhile, Dan was just finishing up fixing his dinner. The thought came to him that he should invite José to eat with him. Ruefully, he looked at the pot of curried garbanzos. He had made just enough for himself. He was very hungry and knew how much food it would take to fill up every corner of his empty stomach. But the thought was persistent, so he went to my office and invited José, who was just packing up his tools.

José gladly accepted the invitation. It was around 8:30 PM, and he hadn't eaten since noon. So while José finished cleaning up, Dan went back to the kitchen, carefully dividing the precious garbanzos into two equal servings. When he was satisfied they were even, he noticed about a tablespoon of beans left in the bottom of the pot. He was just about to put it into his mouth when he heard, "Give it to José." Reluctantly, he dropped the beans into José's bowl. Then he heard, "You won't be hungry."

Sometimes, God fills an obedient child with food that comes from doing His will. As Jesus said when Satan tempted Him to meet His own needs outside the will of God, "Man does not live by bread alone, but by every word that comes from the mouth of God." So that night, even after eating only half of what it usually took to fill him up, Dan was not hungry—just as God had said. And both of these godly men had an enriching time of fellowship that fed their spirits with the nourishment that only God can give.

Carol's Surprise

Carol had been putting off shredding papers, and now there was a big stack of mail on the desk of her home office. On top was an envelope that looked like an ad for something. She told me, "The thought came to me to open it before I shredded it. Inside was a check for $1,185. I thought, *What?* I didn't know if it was real or not."

When I took it to my bank, I told the teller the story. She held the check in front of a scanner and said, "It's good."

Now, a check for more than eleven hundred dollars is good to have, particularly when you're someone who frequently feeds people who can't possibly pay you back. (Recently, it was a single mom with five kids.) Carol also hosts evacuees from fires (including me), visitors from out of town, and others who need a temporary place to stay. But the supernatural part of this story is much more wonderful than the blessing of not shredding a check for a lot of money. It lies in the relationship Carol has with her Savior, the Good Shepherd, who says, *"My sheep know My voice."* He can simply nudge her, and she responds. And, when you think of it, there's something wonderful in His loving care for each one of His children. He knew what was in the envelope and that it was on the stack of papers waiting to be shredded.

If it seems far-fetched to you to think about God knowing the contents of an envelope destined for destruction, remember— He's God. He knows all things at all times. And He's interested in your life and what concerns you.

I think the miracle here is not that the check showed up or that God knew what was in it—it's that Carol felt nudged to open the envelope and did, looking inside even though she thought it was merely more advertising. She could have disregarded the nudge and fed the envelope into the shredder, but she has had years of those nudges and knows it's best to find out what is there beyond her own ideas or how things seem to be.

When we live each day in communion with Almighty God, listening to His voice, guided by His eye, surprising things happen—and we get to participate and be blessed.

Jason's Call

Jason *just happened* to call this morning. He *just happened* to be driving home because they had a plumbing problem, and he had to be there to oversee it. He called me because he *just happened* to see my email, which had *just happened* to arrive on his phone a few minutes before. It was an article on foods that detoxify the liver that I *just happened* to forward to him this morning, though I don't usually deal with emails that early in the day.

Jason is one of my precious prayer partners, and we'd been praying about some health problems he'd been having, so I wanted him to have the information in case there was something that would be helpful in getting him healthy again.

Meanwhile, I was having health problems of my own. They were so troubling that yesterday, I cried out to the Lord, asking for help. I am very careful with my food—organic and non-GMO, gluten-free, and no processed sugar. I reviewed my past meals and found nothing unusual or even different. So why the sudden blurry vision, foggy brain, loss of names and words, and overwhelming fatigue?

I was having my breakfast and getting ready to read my Bible when Jason *just happened* to call. I don't usually answer my phone until after I've finished my quiet time with the Lord, but Jason doesn't call in the morning unless it's an emergency, so I answered.

When I asked if there was something wrong we needed to pray about, he said he just wanted to say hi. He had time and was thinking of me because he *just happened* to see my email come in while he was driving home to deal with the plumbing repairs. He told me to go back to my breakfast and have a good day.

But he and I had recently prayed about some persistent, severe insomnia he was having, so I asked him for an update. He said God had led him to information revealing that fungus in the body can create his symptoms, and he *just happened* to have a natural remedy on hand. He took it, and last night, he'd had the best night's sleep in months.

I told him it was God that he *just happened* to call today and tell me those things because I was having odd symptoms of my own. He asked, "Could the leaks you've been having in your house be causing fungus or mold?" Immediately, I knew it was mold—black mold—highly toxic and dangerous. I felt sure this was the answer, and it *just happened* to come the morning after I cried out to the Lord for help.

Of all the people I could have told about my health problems, Jason *just happened* to be the only one who could have helped me in this way. Years ago, he had studied natural medicine with a naturopath, so he was very familiar with the kinds of remedies that aren't available in health food stores. Immediately, he told me he was going to send me one for black mold.

I thanked Jason for his call, his remedy, and his prayers. I thanked the Lord for this timely answer. I also thanked Him for the plumbing problem that caused Jason to have to make the trip home and for nudging him to give me a call just to say "Hi."

It's another little miracle, and I'm in awe of our God, Who *just happens* to be a very present help in trouble and a loving Father who hears the cries of His children—always.

Wind and Fire

Years ago, my friend Carol was living in a house with a picturesque view of Clear Lake, right across the street. It was a charming house in a lovely location, but there was some concern when she and her husband discovered that the insulation under the house was a mess. They figured there must have been flooding at some point.

That thought came back to her when winter storms hit the area with drenching rains and powerful winds that drove high waves over the banks of the lake. Soon, water was covering the street and creeping up the sloping lawn that surrounded the house.

Alarmed, Carol went outside and commanded the wind and the waves, "Settle down in the name of Jesus!" Then she turned and went back into the house. A little later, she went out again and found the lake perfectly calm.

When I asked what she thought about that, she said, "I freaked out! It scared me!"

I can see why she reacted like that. It's one thing to read the account of Jesus commanding the wind and the waves during a storm while in a little boat with His disciples. We accept that the Creator of the air and the waters has the authority to tell them what to do. It's another thing to command them yourself in the 21st century—and have them obey you. Even though Jesus told us we would do what He did and more, it's still a shock to find out He wasn't kidding.

Years passed, and droughts came. The lake was so low you could walk on mud beneath the docks. In the county next to us, Mendocino Lake was reduced to a puddle, and rivers became trickles—or nothing at all.

I remember a local pastor calling for forty days of fasting and prayer. On the 40th day of the fast, there was rain. It wasn't even the rainy season, but there it was—real rain, not just a sprinkle making spots in the dust on your car.

More rain followed. Lots of it. The lake began to fill up. The rivers began to run. Nobody complained because everyone was relieved that the water table was rising, the wells were filling, and Clear Lake and other lakes in the region were returning to their normal levels.

But then the winds came. By then, Carol had moved to a little community right on the marina, where her backyard gate opened onto the walkway that bordered the lake. High waves were bashing the floats, and it seemed the water would soon be coming into her yard.

She went outside and once more commanded, "Be still in Jesus' name!" And it was. This time, she did not freak out. She told Debra and me, and we rejoiced together.

I don't remember how many years passed between that incident and when the wildfires came—the worst in California history at the time. Five years of them. Hot winds drove the flames, and huge areas were burned to the ground.

At one point, the winds were so strong that they were driving the fires out of control at a furious speed. Firefighters were called in from everywhere, yet the fires could not be contained.

The national forest lies in the north, just above Nice and Lucerne, and the wildfire there was raging. I have friends who live up there. My dear prayer partner Elizabeth lives in Lucerne and my friend Dale lives in Nice

I was worried. If the fire came through the pass, many small towns would burn. The undergrowth was tinder-dry, and there were plenty of trees in the lovely communities at that end of the lake.

But I remembered what Carol had done when the wind was whipping the waves toward her home. So I decided to try it. I went out onto my back deck and said, "Peace! Be still in Jesus' name!"

I live many miles from the north area, so I had no idea what was happening up there. From my deck, the trees were still whipping in the wind. But then Dale called and said, "Up here, not a leaf is stirring."

On Sunday, I was in the prayer circle after the service and shared what Dale had said. Elizabeth, who is a reporter, told me what she had heard from the fire chief.

She said the fire chief had described a small fire that had started near Lucerne. He said the fire's movement was very unusual. It was a "backing fire," meaning it was backing up the hill instead of progressing forward. It was also moving into the wind. He said they had gotten lucky—if the winds had been higher and the fire had been throwing sparks, they wouldn't have been able to contain it so quickly.

At the time, I didn't even know about the small fire. I had been praying about the big one just above Lucerne. For that one, Elizabeth had her own story.

"We had to flee from our home as we watched the fire come over the hills in Lucerne," she said. "I was terrified that our community—our home, the Lucerne Hotel, our neighbors' homes—would be decimated. We simply didn't know what was going on. We managed to gather our pets and some of our most treasured possessions and evacuate to a friend's home for several days.

"By Saturday, we knew everything had survived, but we were still in a breathless state of uncertainty because the fire was still active on the ridges above Lucerne. That evening, I got a call from a man I know. He told me he was going to speak with a priest friend to pray about the fire—to ask that the winds blow away from Lucerne. 'The winds are accessible,' he said. And they were, because that night, the winds blew the fire away from Lucerne."

When I heard that others had been moved to pray about the winds, I knew Jesus had nudged more of His children to ask in His name, in His authority, as His representatives on Earth. And perhaps they were as astonished as I was when the winds turned the fires away.

The Lost Shoe

For years, Stephanie and I had wanted to go to the Monterey Bay Aquarium, but we were both very busy, and she was even more so now that she was a young mother. However, my sight was getting worse, and finally, we decided we had to set a date and go.

When we pulled into the parking lot, Stephanie noticed a woman loading her toddler into a stroller. They were pretty far away, but my friend took a moment to look at them carefully. She was missing her own baby girl and enjoyed seeing the little family. Also, being an artist, she always wanted to observe what people looked like.

The little family was heading for the entrance when Stephanie saw something fall from the stroller. It was a tiny shoe pink like the outfit the toddler was wearing. It lay on the sidewalk, unretrieved, unmissed.

By the time we reached the shoe, the mom was nowhere in sight. We stood wondering what to do. Should we leave it there and hope the mom would come back for it?

Stephanie paused, asking the Lord what to do. Then she put the shoe into her purse. I asked, "Are you going to leave it at

Lost and Found?"

"No," she said. "I have a feeling I'm going to find her."

The aquarium was a complex of multiple passageways leading to exhibits in many rooms, and every place was crowded with people. Where in that vast facility would we find the mom?

We were nearing the end of all the exhibits, and I was getting concerned. I asked Stephanie again if we should leave the shoe at Lost and Found. What if the mom left? It was so crowded, and we'd been there for hours. There were so many rooms and corridors. What were the chances we'd just happen to find her there? Stephanie said she was sure.

Finally, we reached the very last room. We were standing under the dramatic transparent arched ceiling, watching seawater surge across with each incoming wave. It was like being inside the ocean, the upturned faces of the crowd lit with the pale aqua of sunlight shining through the rushing waters. Stephanie glanced at the crowd and said, "There she is!" Smiling, she eased her way through the spectators to the woman and held up the shoe.

"Here's your shoe," she said. "We found it outside on the sidewalk. It's a blessing from God. He said I would see you and be able to give it to you in person."

The woman looked astonished and exclaimed, "Oh my gosh!" She was rather speechless but looked pleased and amazed.

Afterward, Stephanie told me, "I wasn't sure what to do when I first came upon the little shoe. I had the choice to take it or leave it, and I felt I should take it with me. After I took it, I had complete peace the entire time. I wasn't worried, concerned, or distraught. I was confident that God would take care of it."

Musing a moment, she added, "I thought it was interesting that we had to wait the entire time, till the very end. It wasn't in the middle or at the beginning. I thought we'd see her right away because we weren't that far behind her, but it was the very last room where we saw her. But the whole time, I had confidence that God would take care of it.

"When you get nudges from God, and you act upon them,

you get the evidence that you heard Him because the events come to pass. When you ask the Lord to guide you, lead your life, and specifically lead your day, He does."

Timing

My long-time friend and creative partner, Dan, has adjusted my access technology so I am able to continue writing books because my computer will read my words to me. That also means whatever I'm working on can be heard by anyone who happens to be in the room.

So Dan overheard some of Stephanie's baby shoe story. He wasn't impressed. He said it wasn't a miracle. I said no, that was a blessing. The miracle wasn't that the woman showed up; it was another example of how a life can be lived in communion with God, and His directions can be proven by the results of trusting what He said.

I think it's miraculous that God cares about our little lives, knows when a toddler's shoe is lost, and means for its return to be a blessing to the one who lost it and had perhaps little hope of finding it again. The mom seemed so surprised when Stephanie said God told her she would find her. Maybe it touched her that God would do such a thing for her. There wasn't any evidence that she knew Him, and maybe it was a beautiful revelation of His personal love for her.

Dan still wasn't impressed. He said what was more amazing was when our friend Carol got out of her car at the bank and found a packet of thousands of dollars lying in the parking space next to where she pulled up. She said it was stuffed with hundred-dollar bills, though she didn't count them. She told us she paused for a moment and asked, "Lord, is this a blessing?" Then, deciding it wasn't, she went into the bank and handed it to one of the tellers. The teller said they would know whose it was because they had records and timestamps and would be able to contact the owner.

Dan said anyone could have found that packet and kept it.

Who would have known? But God had Carol pull up right after it was dropped. In fact, she said she had seen a well-dressed young man get into an expensive SUV and pull out of that space just as she drove in. She guessed it belonged to him.

"It would have been awful for that man to lose that money," Dan said. "It might have been his life's savings, or money he was going to put toward a wedding ring, or to stop a foreclosure, or something crucial for which he needed cash. But the Lord had Carol turn it in, and the disaster was averted."

We don't know what cascade of horrors might have been loosed by the loss of that money, but when we do what God says— when we don't steal, when we love our neighbor as ourselves, when we choose for the benefit of the other person—our hearts are clean, and the world is a better place.

Divine intervention with perfect timing. God is so good at it. I can think of so many stories where timing was crucial, both in my own life and in the lives of people I know. One of the most stunning is something a classmate told me as I sat on the couch beside him at guide dog school.

Michael Hingson and his associate, David, were setting up for a sales presentation to clients interested in data storage. The system was very expensive, but known for its excellence, so they were confident about their presentation. They had done it many times. Michael's guide dog, Roselle, snoozed peacefully nearby.

Suddenly, there was a heavy jolt, a loud crash, things fell, and heavy furniture slid across the floor as their building violently rocked and swayed. They had no idea what had happened, but when David looked out the window, he told Michael he saw a lot of burning papers falling from above.

Immediately, Michael asked God for direction as he and David hastily began the careful shutdown sequence required to protect the equipment. Then, abruptly, both men felt they had to leave without delay.

Michael grabbed the handle of Roselle's harness, and the three of them rushed to the central stairwell. Michael said he could smell jet fuel as they made the long descent—seventy-eight floors. They stepped into the street only a few minutes before the whole building collapsed in a catastrophe of thick gray ash and smoke.

There were several crucial choices that saved their lives that September eleventh, including which way to turn when they left the burning building, but the timing began with God's nudges early that morning. Michael said if they had continued the mandatory shutdown procedures before leaving the office, they would still have been in the stairwell when the tower came down.

All of his life, Michael has asked the Lord to direct his steps. That terrible day, standing bewildered and confused on the street with chaos all around him, he heard God's voice directing him to run with Roselle. Instantly, he obeyed, and she guided him—along with David and other people blinded by the thick, choking cloud—until she turned into a subway tunnel where there was uncontaminated air and they could breathe again.

There was timing involved, direction required, and comfort afterward as Jesus assured Michael He had saved his life because He had something for him to do. He was not to feel guilty that he'd survived when many others had not. God is sovereign.

When I begin to be ensnared in the cares of this life, Jesus reminds me not to worry. He tells me,

"You don't know the first thing about tomorrow. But I do. And I'll be with you. Trust Me no matter what it looks like. I'm holding you and all your tomorrows in My hand, and My timing is perfect."

Head-on

For several frustrating hours, Carol had been dealing with mishap after mishap and logistics that required several phone calls before she got everything worked out. It had severely delayed her scheduled departure, but finally, she was on her way home. Three hours to go.

At least it was a clear afternoon and there was no traffic. As Carol started on a fairly straight two-lane stretch of Highway 29, a sedan passed her. She was several car lengths behind when she noticed the sedan drifting toward the center line. She thought the driver would correct his car, but he didn't. He crossed the center line and raced along in the oncoming lane.

Carol told me, "When I saw the car ahead of me actually driving in the oncoming lane, I slowed down and said urgently, 'Jesus, Jesus, Jesus, no, no, no, no, no, no. This can't be!' I couldn't believe my eyes. Could not believe it. I knew something was bound to happen. I kept slowing down, and almost instantly, a white vehicle came around the bend—and the two cars hit head on. Kaboom! By then, I was stopped in my lane.

"I sat there as the big white vehicle rolled violently to my left and the small sedan rolled to my right. It all was instant. Could not believe my eyes. I was amazed I was sitting there untouched. *What do I do, Lord?* I started driving, called 911. Could hardly breathe or speak."

By the time Carol neared Kelseyville, emergency vehicles were already on their way. She was still in shock. "There was no reason for those two cars not to plow right into me," she said. "I was just sitting there. One car went off to the right like crazy—dust was flying everywhere—and the other car went off the other way.

"The Lord said, *'Yes, I saved your life.'* It was not His will for my life to end, especially not like that!"

That night, Carol checked the CHP reports and found the accident listed. It said "No injuries." She couldn't believe that. The cars had been rolling violently after a head-on collision. Having been in the mortuary business, she figured the report was written that way to protect the families.

A couple of days later, she drove to the place that does the towing. She told the tow truck driver, "I was right behind the accident on Highway 29 Tuesday night, and the report said there were no injuries." And he said, "That's right."

Carol was astonished. "I thought the two cars were totally

demolished and nobody could survive it. I told him the whole thing is a miracle of God, and he said, 'Yes, it is.' He said there were two young guys in the small sedan. They had been out drinking and were joyriding. That's how they ended up in the wrong lane. In the white vehicle, there was one guy. The tow truck driver said he ended up taking the three of them home, so I think they must have been all right."

I truly believe Carol's prayer made a significance difference that night. We are not meant to be mere spectators on earth, impotent bystanders watching in horror while fires rage, winds roar, and cars crash. When we see something wrong, we can do something about it. We're in partnership with God. Sometimes He intervenes with protection. Sometimes it's with prevention. In Carol's case, it was both. We don't passively observe; we participate. We pray.

The Woman on the Road

It was 10:30 at night as Dan was driving home on a country highway—one of those without streetlights and only one lane going in each direction. At that hour, it was pretty deserted, but he spotted a small pickup ahead going slower than he wanted. The road was clear and straight, so he stepped on the gas to pass.

He was up to sixty or seventy miles per hour, looking in the side-view mirror to make sure it was safe to merge back into his lane, when he caught sight of something out of the corner of his eye. It was a young woman walking in the middle of the oncoming lane. He panicked and cranked the wheel hard to the right, missing the girl by about three inches. It was so close that he could see the blank, expressionless look on her face.

Dan shuddered with the memory. "She was walking toward me in the center of the other lane," he said. "If I had hit her, she would have come through my windshield. It was a miracle that I saw her and was able to react in time. God was really watching out for both of us. I could easily have splattered her.

"It took me a while to get the van under control. It was swaying wildly back and forth from the oversteering, but finally, I was able to pull onto the shoulder of the road. The pickup drove by me and kept going. It was dead quiet after that. I was shaking all over. I was so freaked out. I came within inches of killing that girl, and it could have killed me too.

"I made a U-turn and drove back to the girl. She was still walking in the middle of the road. I was furious. I put on my emergency flashers, got out, and started yelling at her, 'What do you think you're doing? You could have been killed!' She was drunk. She and her boyfriend had been in a fight, and she demanded that he let her out of the car—and he did, right there in the middle of nowhere.

"I was thinking, *What am I going to do with this stupid girl?* I told her she couldn't stay there. She could either get in my car, and I'd take her to town so she could call someone, or we'd stay there until the Highway Patrol came by. She wasn't having any of it. She was belligerent. She said, 'I wish you would've just killed me.'

"I didn't know what to do, except I knew I couldn't leave her there like that."

Right then, the pickup Dan had passed pulled up. It wasn't right away because the man had driven a while before turning around. Dan filled the guy in on what was going on. The man told the girl, "I'm a Christian. I own a motel in town, and my wife is there. You can stay there tonight, and we won't charge you. Things will look clearer in the morning." He was very calm and kind, and she finally agreed to go with him.

Dan said, "The guy had given me his business card, so I called him the next day to check on the girl. He told me, 'My wife and I talked to her, and she's all right. She's going to stay another day, and we'll help her work things out.' He also said, 'I can't believe you didn't lose control and go off the road or flip your car. That was some great driving.'"

It was maybe a year later when Dan got a call from the girl. She had stayed in touch with the man and had gotten Dan's number from him. She said, "Thank you for coming back. Thanks for not hitting me, for pulling over, for making sure I was okay, and for staying with me until that guy helped me. I've rebuilt my life." She was glad she hadn't died that night.

She was a speed waterskier, and she had a race that day in Lakeport. Dan said, "She invited me to her meet, but I was too busy with work to go. Still, it was amazing getting a call from her.

"It's a miracle I saw her. It's a miracle I didn't hit her. It's a miracle I didn't flip my car or slam into the pickup. It's a miracle that the Christian guy turned around and came back. He said he just had a feeling he should go back.

"All of this is God. And all of this is miraculous to me."

Omniscient

How can God keep track of so many things at once—respond in compassion to the request of a sick teenager, protect the life of a woman who only wants to die, or answer a plea for a small amount of hamburger? In all the stories in this book, one thing is constant: God is aware of every need, hears every word, and responds in ways that astonish us.

How does He do it? I don't know. The Mind that thought up quantum mechanics and how to combine three atoms to make a substance that sustains all life on Earth—one that can exist as liquid, solid, and vapor—is able to intervene in times, individuals, and circumstances. God knew it would be difficult for us to understand, so He said things about Himself and how He thinks to help us at least get a glimpse of what that means.

"My thoughts are not your thoughts," He says, "nor are your ways My ways. As high as the heavens are above the earth, so much higher are My ways than your ways and My thoughts than your thoughts."

Understatement.

I think one of the reasons God often presents Himself in Scripture as "Creator of heaven and earth and the sea and all there is in them" is that it sets our perception of Him in perspective. As Scripture says, He holds the universe in His hand and calls all the stars by name. Are you kidding? Do you know how many stars there are?

I used to think God (if there was one) was much too big and important to bother with us puny, insignificant beings. I decided that if He created everything, He must have set it in motion and gone on to more important matters. Then, after I started finding out who He really is, He told me, "It takes a far bigger God to know every hair on your head and the thoughts and intents of your heart."

Scripture says He knows our downsitting, our uprising, our words before they leave our mouths. Our dark places are not dark to God. Everything is light to Him, and He can bring light into our darkest, most frightening troubles.

It also says He knit us together in our mother's womb, that He wrote every member of our being in His book before there were any of them. He watched over us as we were being formed in secret, intricately embroidered with various colors.

One day, He told me His thoughts toward me are more than the sands—more than every grain. That's how attentive He is to the matters of my life and everything that concerns me. And, at the same time, He's thinking of Carol, Debra, Byron, Dan, Katerina, Kathy, Jason, Nancy, John, Nathan, Michael, Pamela, Stephanie, Bea, Moe, Elizabeth, David, Dale, Anthony, José, everyone else on Earth who has ever been, who is living now, and who is still to be born—and you. And His thoughts toward you and each one of us are also more than the grains of sand.

When He told me the sum of His thoughts toward me was more than the grains of sand, I was shocked by the immensity of His knowing—His caring awareness, His ability to see every need and hear every word, whether a thought, whisper, or cry. It can be unnerving when you realize God knows everything that's going on—all at once, all the time. Past, present, and future— He sees it all simultaneously because He's in the Eternal Now.

For Him, it's always Now.

Even more astounding, He knows every sparrow that falls and tells us we are more important to Him than many sparrows. He invites us to join His family, adopted and accepted as dear children. He says He will be a Father to us and we shall be His sons and daughters. He promises to watch over us always, the Good Father that He is.

But isn't that like being constantly scrutinized for wrongdoing, like surveillance cameras recording every movement, word, and interaction wherever we are?

It's not like that. He's not like that. He's omniscient—all-knowing. It's how He is, not just what He does. He's not some kind of Cosmic Cop or Killjoy. He's God, and omniscience is an aspect of who He is. It goes with another aspect of His being: omnipresence.

He's not in everything, and He is not everything; He just is. He is not His creation. He made it; He's not in it. But somehow, even so, He's also everywhere all the time. If it seems too difficult for your little pea brain, just remember—He's God.

He's Himself, not something people made up to help explain thunder and lightning. He's beyond our understanding. If He weren't, He would be too small. He is Himself, revealed to us in words we can at least somewhat comprehend. But, as He said to Job, even if I told you, you still wouldn't understand. "Couldn't" is probably more accurate.

Even His revealed name, YHWH (Yahweh or Jehovah, with added vowels for pronunciation), is not a noun—it's a verb. Wrap your head around that one. His name is I AM. He's active. He's always working. He's always watching over you.

That's pretty overwhelming, but God, seen in the complexity and entirety of what He says about Himself, is overwhelming. At the same time, He is gracious, merciful, and good.

And if He seems rather intimidating in His power, presence, and total awareness of everything all the time, well, a little awe, respect, and fear is appropriate.

He's not our buddy or "The Man Upstairs." He's a consuming fire, King of the Universe, Judge of all the Earth. Someday, each one of us will stand before Him and give an account of our lives.

Solomon, the wisest man of all time, wrote, "The fear of the Lord is the beginning of wisdom."

Perhaps "fear" is better stated as "solemn regard." It's wise to take Him seriously because He is Almighty God, and He knows what He's talking about. When He tells you something, it's because you need to know it—and it's meant to keep you safe and make your life better. It's always for your good. It always gives you life, not futility and dead ends.

His is a benevolent watching over us because He is love.

Yes, the Lord of everything loves you. He doesn't make anything He doesn't love, and He keeps loving you all your days.

It's who He is.

There's not a part of your life that God's not interested in. You matter that much to Him.

And if you're still worried that He's just waiting for you to mess up so He can squish you, here's what He says about His thoughts toward you—which are more than all the grains of sand:

"I know the thoughts I have toward you, plans for good and not for evil, to give you a future and a hope."

Part 3

Sophie

Sophie and her husband, Jim, had just moved to California with their two little boys and not much else. Far from friends and family, they felt alone and unsure of what to do next when an ulcer developed on Jim's foot. It was so bad he had to go to the hospital, but even after he'd been there nearly a month, the doctors hadn't been able to get it to heal.

Sophie had no idea what to do. Some time before, her cousin had given her a Bible, but she had never read it. Desperate, she picked it up and started looking through the pages for something that would comfort her. Tears ran down her face, and her heart cried out to the God she'd heard about in the Catholic church when she was a little girl but had ignored in favor of a life she thought would be more fun and fulfilling. It had not gone well. "Please, God," she cried, "give me something to make me feel better."

The phone rang. It was the hospital. A doctor was telling her that the ulcer had gone to the bone. If it didn't heal soon, they would have to amputate Jim's foot. That threw her into total panic.

Just then, there was a knock at the door. When Sophie opened it, she saw a tall man who introduced himself as Pastor Fredrickson. He said he had been visiting people at the hospital, and Jim had asked him to check on her and the boys, so she invited him in. He looked at her and said, "I can see you're upset." Then he reached into his pocket and pulled out a Bible. "Here," he said, "let me read you something that will make you feel better."

Sophie was so stunned she couldn't even speak. Only moments before, she had been weeping, imploring God to give her something that would help her feel better, and here was this man who said the very same words she had just said to God. Jesus had heard Sophie, who had ignored Him, run away, and chosen to pursue all the things she knew the Bible said not to do—and yet, He heard her prayer.

Miracles followed, including the healing of Jim's foot, but the greatest healing miracle was what happened in Sophie's broken heart on that day of hopeless despair. When she took the ugly, tangled mess of her life and gave it all to Jesus, He gave her His forgiveness and a brand-new start.

Sophie told me it was extremely difficult for her to walk with God instead of depending upon herself, but someone gave her a scripture that she grabbed onto and has lived by ever since:

"Trust in the Lord with all your heart and lean not on your own understanding. Acknowledge Him in all your ways, and He will direct your path."

Acknowledge Him. Be aware that He is right there with you. He, who knows the beginning from the end, who can see what's far ahead as well as what's right before your feet this very minute, will show you the way to go and guide your steps in the path of peace.

John's Lost Job

God always wants the best for us, though at times it may not look like it. Sometimes, like Sophie, we find ourselves in a chaos of catastrophes because He respects our free will so truly that He is willing to let us do what we feel is right in our own eyes. And yet, when we ask Him for help, He is there to pull us out of the pit and heal our broken lives.

And sometimes He provides for us by meeting our needs in ways that make no sense to us. Such was the case in this story my son John told me.

"My wife was pregnant with our third child, but we were managing because I was working. Then we had a six-month layoff, and that in itself was inconvenient timing since a new member of the family is expensive. Then, when our daughter was born, we found out she was deaf. Not only did we have the expenses of a new baby, but we also had the added costs of getting her tested, getting her hearing aids, and covering all the other expenses associated with caring for a deaf child.

"I thought, *God, why in the world would You get me laid off from work when I have all these things coming up and I can't pay for them?*

"I knew I was really going to struggle to cover those added expenses, even with the help of the insurance provided by my job—and now even that was gone. But God had a different way of meeting our needs. In Oregon, unemployed parents can get coverage through the Oregon Health Plan, and it covers medical issues, especially things like hearing aids. Oregon Health Plan covered all of our daughter's testing, her hearing aids, her speech therapy, and all of the services she received because God, in His wisdom, took away my job before she was born."

God does all things well. As Dan says, "It works out for the best in the end. We just don't always see the end."

The Baby Next Door

Forty-eight years ago, when I was a brand-new Christian, I lived next door to a lovely young couple with a baby, and they were Christians too.

One day, the mom brought her baby to me and asked if I would pray for him. She said he'd had diarrhea for three days. She had taken him to the doctor, but the medicine hadn't helped.

I had never prayed for anyone, much less such an unhappy child, but I said okay.

If I had had any idea of what to say, it went out of my head as soon as she placed the squirming infant into my arms. I had expected that as I began to pray over him, the baby would settle into sniffles and then into a peaceful sleep.

It didn't happen. I managed to mumble out a few things while I tried to keep hold of the thrashing child. His cries did not diminish, nor did his writhing. Embarrassed, I handed him back to his mom. She thanked me and disappeared into her house.

That didn't go well, I said to myself. I'd heard stories of people who prayed for the sick, and, as in the Book of Acts, the lame walked, and the blind received their sight. Apparently, I was not the "Rise and walk!" kind of Christian.

The next day, I happened to see the mom out in her yard. She came over and, with a big smile, told me that in the night, her baby had stopped crying—and so had the diarrhea.

That's when I learned one of the most important truths of the Christian life. Prayer is not magic words—a cosmic command that causes something miraculous to take place; it's a request to the God of the Universe, the Most High, All-knowing, All-wise One to intervene on our behalf. It wasn't my great faith that healed the child; it was faith in my great God. All I had to do was ask. He did the rest.

Phyllis

My friend Carol deeply loved her mother-in-law, Phyllis, and they enjoyed a close relationship. Carol and her husband, Mike, took care of her in their home until she started having health issues. They moved her to a nursing home so she could get the medical help she needed.

"We were worried about her," Carol said. "She was in her early eighties, and the situation was dire. The doctor said she was in kidney failure. Then we got the call that they had to send her to the emergency room. On the drive down there, Mike and I prayed, 'Lord, don't let her die before she is saved.'"

"She was on a gurney in the emergency room, and only one of us could go in at a time, so Mike went in first. After he came out, I went in and said, 'Phyllis, what are you doing here? What's going on?'

"And she said, 'I've been waiting for you.'

"I said, 'Phyllis, I don't want you to die without knowing for sure you're going to heaven.'

"She said, 'Me either. What do I do?'

"I prayed for her, and she received the Lord, and that dear

elderly woman was born again."

"Easter came. We took her to church, and then she wanted to go over to the coast. The doctor said she didn't have long because of her kidney failure. So we went to the coast and stayed overnight. The next morning, we sat Phyllis in a chair, and Mike and I prayed for her.

"We had been hearing about a lot of healings happening around the country, so Mike and I had prayed together, 'Lord, we would love to pray ourselves and see someone healed.'

"So that day at the coast, we prayed for Phyllis because it was the right thing to do. We didn't feel any special anointing. We sat her in the chair and said, 'Lord, would You please heal Phyllis of her kidney failure?' It was very simple. On Monday, we took her back to the nursing home.

"On Wednesday, I went there to see her, and as I was walking by the desk to go to her room, one of the girls at the desk said, 'Carol, we can't believe it. Phyllis's blood work is normal.'

"I said, 'What?'

"And she said, 'Her blood work is normal. She no longer has kidney failure.'

"I said, 'Oh my gosh! God healed her!'

"And the gal said, 'What?'

"I said, 'We prayed for her, and God healed her.'

"Phyllis was no longer in kidney failure, and she lived about three more years after that. God is so good. He loves to love on us. He loves to surprise us"

Katie's Injury

"Katie fell today!" Irma's face was full of anguish. "She stepped off a curb wrong and fell. She can't walk. She's in a lot of pain and has to stay in bed. I want you to come with me and pray for her."

I wasn't sure what I could do to help, but my roommate was insistent. So right after dinner, we hastily made our way through the corridors to Katie's room. She was lying very still on her bed, her foot covered with ice packs. Quietly, Katie's roommate told us X-rays showed torn ligaments and a chipped bone. Her foot wouldn't support her weight, and she couldn't even make it to the bathroom by herself.

Katie opened her eyes. They were dark with pain and sadness. She told me her dog was the perfect guide for her—a small yellow Lab so responsive she didn't need correction. Katie was struggling to hold back tears. Hoarsely, she said, "If I leave now, I won't get to keep Penelope. She'll go back in the string and be given to someone else."

I had no idea what to say. The instructors at Guide Dogs for the Blind were also the ones who trained the dogs. They were careful to match each guide with the client whose needs and personality it suited best. Since that unique partnership of guide dog and blind person was usually about ten years, it was absolutely crucial that they suited one another. Otherwise, the bond of loving trust that must be formed would not be complete. I stood silently in the grief of Katie's loss, waiting for Irma to pray for our classmate.

Abruptly, Irma announced, "Carolyn's going to pray now, okay, Katie?"

Katie closed her eyes and nodded.

What? I thought Irma was going to pray. I had agreed to come and give moral support. What could I say in the wake of this overwhelming catastrophe?

But they were waiting. I took a deep breath and launched out, hoping to bring some kind of comfort and encouragement in this hopeless situation. I prayed for the foot, of course, but I was more concerned about Katie's grief. I prayed for peace of heart. And then, my most relied-upon Bible verse, Romans 8:28: *"God works all things together for good for those who love Him and are His."*

When my mother was so ill, I lived off that Scripture. I told Katie I didn't know how Jesus could turn an incurable, relentless degenerative neurological disease to good, but He did. And it wasn't just, "Oh, that's nice." It was WOWIE-ZOWIE, blow-your-socks-off Good. I said I didn't know how He would do that for her, but He was an expert at changing the worst to the best. I prayed that He would glorify Himself in the matter and left Katie's room, wondering what that might mean.

The next day, I happened to be waiting at the nurse's office when Katie's roommate rushed in. Breathlessly, she blurted, "This morning, Katie got up and made it into the bathroom all by herself! Yesterday, she couldn't even stand up, much less walk! She said it didn't hurt as much and she wants to stay!"

That was the start of a series of surprises that culminated in Katie's walk across the graduation stage three weeks later to receive the leash from the hand of Penelope's puppy raiser. That was pretty WOWIE-ZOWIE Good in itself, but it was even more astonishing when I learned that the examinations and subsequent X-rays had revealed not a chipped bone but a broken metatarsal—an injury they said would have taken at least six months to heal. That blew my socks off.

Somehow, Jesus had turned the worst to the best. And perhaps those who witnessed that miracle saw, if only for a moment, that God is real and that He hears and answers prayers in ways that can't be explained—except as the divine intervention of One who loves us more than we can possibly imagine.

Healing Prayers

The Bible says the fervent prayer of a righteous person avails much. And Jesus said to more than one healed person, "Your faith has made you well." No doubt about it, Jesus responded to fervent faith. He heard blind Bartimaeus crying out at the top of his lungs and the woman who pressed through the crowd, hoping just to touch the hem of His garment.

But what I love about the three previous accounts of healing prayers in this book is that the ones speaking the prayers were anything but fervent. We were just asking, and we weren't even particularly expecting anything miraculous to happen. But it did—because we asked and because God wanted to.

In case you've heard that people don't get healed because they didn't have enough faith or had sin in their lives, I ask you—where was the faith and fervency in anyone in the funeral procession when Jesus called the widow's son back to life? Certainly not the widow, the mourners, or the corpse. Or when Lazarus had been dead for four days? Not even Mary and Martha, who were Jesus' friends and whom He loved dearly, showed any faith that He would heal their dead brother.

Even the case I mentioned in Part 1, about the little boy who got new eyeballs—miraculous as that was—turned out not to be God's response to the man's powerful prayer. Instead, when the man finished telling me his story, God pointed out to me that the prayer had been hesitant and full of disclaimers, absolutely not a demonstration of deep and confident faith. God said an angel had to talk him into praying. No, it wasn't the man's faith. God said, "I healed the boy because I wanted to so badly."

Now, we all know of cases where a person did not get healed, no matter how fervently people prayed. God is still sovereign. But I included these three little stories because there is no incantation, no particular level of faith, no certain set of words that obligates God to heal someone. But if you ask, He might just surprise you with a 'Yes.' And if you don't ask, the answer will always be 'No.'

Caleb

My young friend Caleb is an experienced actor, singer, dancer, and choreographer. He spent several years in Los Angeles appearing in plays, movies, commercials, and even an opera. Recently, he moved back to Kansas, where most of his family lives, but he still has connections in L.A., where casting can be a matter of getting to the studio whenever they say.

A few Mondays ago, Caleb received a call for a job—a commercial—and they wanted him there at 10:00 AM the next day. Last-minute plane tickets are expensive, but a friend with a lot of frequent flyer miles offered to cover his flight. It looked as if God was opening the way for him to get there fast. The first problem was solved.

But there were others. He would have to be there for three days. That meant finding a place to stay and transportation, and all of this needed to be arranged quickly.

Meanwhile, my friend Christy was praying. She doesn't try to control or direct her son's life, but she always covers him in prayer. When Caleb told her about this opportunity, she immediately began praying. As her son hurried to get things worked out, Christy was asking God about it—and in this matter, she had no peace.

Then she got a weather warning that high winds were expected in L.A. She told Caleb about the forecast without mentioning the lack of peace in her spirit. He said he wasn't going. Though he had tried everything he could think of, he hadn't been able to get the logistics to work out.

The next day, hot, dry Santa Ana winds hit L.A., and fires started. At ninety miles an hour, driving, raging fires wiped out whole communities in minutes.

And Caleb was not there.

I don't know if, on Monday night, Caleb felt discouraged, thwarted in his attempts to answer a call that would have meant another opportunity to use his skills in the difficult, competitive field he had chosen for himself. Maybe he wondered if God was deliberately making things difficult. Whatever he was feeling that evening, I bet he felt different on Tuesday morning when the worst fires in California history blazed uncontrollably, and so much that had been glorious and impressive was now in ashes.

Sometimes people say, "God heard me and answered my prayer." That could give you the impression that God doesn't always hear us and only answers certain prayers. But God always hears us when we talk to Him, and He always answers. It's not an answer only when things happen that we ask for.

Chuck Smith, the founder of Calvary Chapel, said God always chooses for our good. It's just that we want our *temporal* good, and He always wants our *eternal* good.

Christian musician and singer Bryan Duncan said God has three answers to prayer: "Yes," "Not yet," and "I have something better."

And my friend Bob Cull (Bea Cull was his grandmother) told me, "No is as good an answer as yes if you know His heart."

God always does what is best for us. In the case of my friend Caleb and the job he couldn't get to, it's a good thing he wasn't in L.A. at 10:00 AM on Tuesday morning.

So, if it seems you have been thwarted in a heart's desire—if you're discouraged and feeling defeated because you can't move ahead or make things work out—maybe God is saving you from being caught in devastating, uncontrollable fires, in whatever form they may take. As He has told me more than once when I was the most discouraged, "When you know why, you'll be glad."

Not for Sissies

When Jesus rescued me in 1977, I was totally ignorant of all things Christian. I had been brought up Taoist/Confucian— two philosophies of how life works and how to conduct yourself in it. I had no concept of God, a Creator, or the Bible. I was as clueless as an atheist that there was anything beyond this present earthly existence.

In the 1980s, there were a lot of teachings along the lines of "Name It, Claim It" or, as some have called it, "Blab It, Grab It." The church I attended taught that nothing bad would ever happen to you if you were obedient. If you were sick, it was evidence that there was sin in your life. I once heard the pastor's wife angrily shout at a little boy, "You're so disobedient that if you ran out into the street right now, a truck would hit you because Jesus wouldn't protect you."

We were taught that prosperity was evidence of pleasing God. Jesus wanted us to be healthy, wealthy, and wise. If we weren't, well, Jesus was punishing us so we'd get back in line.

In my ten years at that church, I don't remember ever hearing a message on the Book of Job. Not surprisingly, when I began reading it on my own, I couldn't see anything wrong with the arguments of Job's friends. Surely, Job had done something that deeply offended God. Why else would he lose everything, including his health?

Not only is that doctrine false, it's also damaging and dangerous. Those who are taught that God promises an abundant life according to human standards are mystified or offended when things go wrong. *If God is omnipotent, He could have stopped this. If God is good, if He is love, why are these terrible things happening?*

Unfortunately, the prosperity doctrine persists to this day. Where does that leave those of us being crushed under the rising cost of everything? According to that doctrine, we're not believing God enough, not pure enough, not obedient enough... But the truth is, Jesus never promised us an easy life. The Christian life is not for sissies. It means trusting Him to be there in every circumstance, no matter what happens. It means seeing the whole Big Picture, not just what is directly in front of our physical eyes.

Meanwhile, things continue to look pretty bad at times. Jesus Himself went through suffering. And after He left, Nero was Caesar. He liked to have Christians drenched in oil and set on fire to light up his garden parties.

Jesus knew very well what the world was like, and He told His disciples, *"In this world, you will have tribulation—you'll have trials, distress, and frustration."*

And in the midst of it all, He called them to live in a way entirely different from everyone else. He wanted them to love their enemies, bless those who cursed them, and pray for those who slandered, reviled, and lied about them. He asked them to forgive—to love others as much as they loved themselves. Yes, He knew it was difficult. For human beings, it was more than difficult—it was impossible. But with Him, nothing was impossible. When they surrendered their lives to Him, all things became possible. It was supernatural, and it was theirs if they let Him lead.

He promised they would see life in a whole new way. Would they rather be caterpillars or butterflies? That was the difference between life on their own and life with Him as King. He would give them the inner strength to persevere, endure, and overcome. He would guide them when the road was long and full of hills and holes, and He would give them the ability to see things from His perspective—far higher than human understanding. He would enable them to face trials the world called insurmountable, and if they allowed Him to work through those trials, He would reveal opportunities that would cause them to emerge with hearts full of praise.

Jesus never promised everything would be easy, but He said, *"Take heart. Be of good courage. Don't come unglued, don't be anxious, cowardly, or faint in the day of adversity. Though your strength is small, lean on Me. I have overcome the world. I have deprived it of power to harm you."*

When He gave His own life to die in our place, He broke the power of sin's ability to enslave us. The shackles are off. The prison door is open. We are now free to live a whole different way—as different from what we had before as paper is to fire.

When I escaped the warped version of Christianity I had thought was the truth, I had a lot to overcome. I was suicidal for a year and a half, and every day was a struggle. Every day I had to decide if I still wanted to live another day. I was so devastated. For ten years, I thought I was following the One who is the Way, the Truth, and the Life. For ten years, I had been deep in the exertions required to please the glowering Ancient of Days, who was never satisfied because I was never doing enough, never good enough, and, ultimately, never enough.

Actually, that's true. We aren't good enough. We can never be good enough. But we don't have to be. It's not about how good we can be; it's about how good He is. That's why it's so mind-blowing that Jesus let me give Him my shattered life, wrapped me in His love, and gave me Himself. He forgave all my failings. Then He welcomed me into His family, fresh as a newborn child.

Did that make my life easy? No. As I said before, the Christian life is not for sissies. It's very different to live in a place with another kind of gravitational pull. You have to learn a whole new way to walk in a world you grew up thinking you knew how to navigate.

Jesus knew it would be a big adjustment for us to be spiritually awakened human beings still living on a fallen Earth. He wanted us to know so we wouldn't have unrealistic expectations—no whitewash, no sugar-coating. Sometimes, life would be beyond our ability to endure, but in our weakness, He would be our strength. And through it all, He promised to be with us— faithful, gracious, aware of our sorrows, and wanting to show us how to deal with them in wholesome, productive ways. *"You will have tribulation,"* He said, *"but trust Me. I have said these things to you so that in Me, you will have perfect peace."*

God does not disable the law of entropy in the lives of His children. We still have leaks in our pipes, ants in our kitchens, rats in our basements, pestilence, injustice, suffering, sorrow, and death. Being a Christian does not make us immune to human life. But this is not all there is. We are part of something far bigger than we can see. The threads of our lives are woven together in the tapestry of all human time. Mostly, we trust it will be beautiful in the end, but right now, as my friend Debra says, the only things we see are knots and some seemingly random bits of color.

On the other side, we will see when God's mystery, His secret design, His hidden purpose is completed. Then we will see clearly how perfectly everything worked together in that supernatural partnership between humanity and the Omniscient, Omnipotent, Omnipresent Almighty God.

Here is a great mystery. Scripture says we are God's workmanship—His *poema*, His work of art, His little masterpiece. It says He created us for good works in Christ Jesus. He made us for a purpose, transformed by our relationship with our Savior.

And here's the most astonishing part: Scripture tells us all of this was prepared by God beforehand. Before the beginning of time, God had you in His heart. He designed you for this specific era of human history. Can you comprehend it?

He also designed, ordained, and set in order good works for you to do—works that benefit others and make their lives better.

When you live for yourself, your life is only as big as you are. But when you know you're part of something much bigger, when you know you're participating in a plan as vast as the cosmos, and when you know the One with whom you're partnering is the Creator of it all—you can have peace in the midst of it. Because He is here. He promised.

The Piano

My dad loved giving presents, always doing so with a flashy flamboyance that would make a big impression on the recipient and all who were around. So it was that when he told me he and Mom were buying me a house, he added magnanimously, "And it comes with a baby grand piano."

I had always wanted a baby grand—shiny, ebony, and elegant, even as it sat silently, gracing the room in which it was placed. I was excited. I particularly liked Young Chang pianos.

The problem was, in this kind of gift-giving, my dad was impulsive, and sometimes after making a generous announcement, he would reconsider and later restate the extravagant gift with added requirements and limitations. I had learned over the years not to hold any promise of this sort too close to my heart.

Mom had been getting progressively weaker with something the doctors were calling Parkinson's Plus. I started going to Southern California regularly to help my dad as he took care of her in their home. He said he had taken vows at their wedding and intended to keep them—for richer, for poorer, in sickness and in health, till death…

So I went every few weeks and helped with whatever was needed as Mom slowly lost more and more function.

During one particular visit, my dad told me we could go shopping for a baby grand, saying, "You have $10,000."

I was dismayed. All the baby grands I knew of, the ones that were worth anything, were at least twice that much. I told him so, but he said there were discount places. I had a horrible vision of him taking me to a shoddy warehouse where crummy pianos with lousy action and tinny voices were displayed. A bad baby grand was worse than none at all. So I told him, but he said that was the limit. I gave up on ever getting a baby grand.

At that time, Mom's hands and arms still worked, so she continued one of her favorite pastimes—reading the newspaper. She said, "Oh, the Chinese acrobats are going to be at the fair this year. I want to go see them."

The L.A. County Fair is one of the biggest in the country. It covers a wide expanse of land and has a lot of very large buildings, each with something wonderful inside, from art to flowers to the latest appliances. That year, the garden building featured life-sized mechanical dinosaurs that moved behind giant ferns. Mom wanted to see that too.

When we got to the gate, I suggested we get a wheelchair so she could ride. Mom declined. She said she didn't want to give in to her weakness. She could still walk, and she was certainly going to do so.

I was alarmed, but I had also been brought up not to dispute a parental decision, so we started on our way to the building where the Chinese acrobats would be performing—which happened to be a long way from the gate.

Mom was going very slowly, and I knew the performance was about to start, so I said I'd go ahead and save seats for them.

Off I dashed, found the building, and heard the music. The acrobats were already performing, and all the folding chairs were filled. I stood behind the last row, looking back at the door often so I could wave my parents over when they arrived.

But they didn't come. Soon the acrobats were gone, and people were moving on. I stood there wondering what to do. I decided to walk back to the entrance, which was all the way across the huge building.

I don't know how long I was there, walking back and forth, searching for my parents in a noisy building packed with strangers crowding around the exhibits. Where could they be? Had something happened to my mom? How would I know? We didn't have cell phones. How would my dad be able to contact me? How would I ever find them again?

From the time I was a little girl, I had a terror of being lost, and recurring dreams of getting separated from my mom. It was my worst nightmare. Even though I was in my forties, I felt like a small child. People were talking loudly, vendors were hawking, music was blaring. I was getting more and more frantic and almost in tears when I finally found a security guard.

"I can't find my mom and dad," I wailed.

In a kindly voice, the guard said the best thing to do was to find one prominent spot and sit down. Stay there. They would be looking for me too. If I kept walking around, we'd never see each other.

Sniffling, I thanked the guard and walked a little farther until I found the first available seat. Though I had traversed the entire building several times and woven through the center section and along all the sides, I had not seen this merchant before. The bench I was sitting on was smooth and glossy black. I turned around and found I was seated at a baby grand. On the front, in sedate golden letters, it said *Young Chang*.

Having nothing else to do, I put my fingers on the keys and played a little. I couldn't hear a thing over the din, but the action felt good. My fingers were at home on them. Nice touch, this Young Chang had—but it could still have a terrible voice. Pianos are a very subjective instrument. If they don't fit the player, there will be little joy in making music.

Then I heard a voice inside my heart. It said, *You'll like it.*

A man came out and asked what I thought of the piano. I told him I couldn't hear a thing, but the action was nice.

Just then, to my great relief, my dad came striding up. "I thought I'd find you with the pianos," he said. I found that interesting since I didn't even know the pianos where there until I sat down in front of one.

"Mom is sitting down over there," he said, gesturing toward the entrance of the building. "She couldn't make it, so they carried her here. She's resting now."

When Daddy went back to tell Mom he'd found me, I told the man my dad had promised to buy me a baby grand, but the limit was $10,000, so this Young Chang was out of the question. I had read the tag. It was not $10,000. It was more. Too much more.

Meanwhile, I asked if the piano did MIDI, explaining that I was working on an album of Scripture songs I'd written, and having MIDI would make it easier to complete. The man said yes, it had a MIDI module. He turned out to be the owner—and a Christian.

He left for a few minutes, and when my dad came back, the owner said it was the last day of the fair, and he didn't want to have to take all the pianos back to his warehouse. He asked my dad if he'd consider buying this piano for $12,000, including shipping to my house.

Soon after I returned home, the Young Chang was there, looking like what a dream come true looks like when the dream really does come true. Carefully, I opened the cover and placed my fingers on the keys. The action was like butter, and the voice was so beautiful it brought tears to my eyes.

In the din and distress of that horrible day at the fair, God had whispered, "*You'll like it.*" And I did. And more. Much more. I loved it.

But there was one more surprise. When I looked inside the piano, I saw the serial number of this particular Young Chang.

It ended with the letters CG—my initials.

Some people would say, "Ah! It was meant to be!" But that feels too much like inevitable, impersonal fate. I see it differently. To me, it says God meant it to be.

It feels like a sweet little kiss from the One who loves me most.

And my mom? After she had rested quite a while, she asked us to take her to see the dinosaurs in the garden building—and she let us push her in a wheelchair.

I still have that beautiful baby grand. It sits in my house, reminding me that God can turn my worst nightmare into a thing of breathtaking beauty—because He is able to make astonishing good come out of the worst circumstances.

Beauty for ashes. It's His specialty.

The Rat Story

Ever since I lost so much of my sight, Dan has been managing my bills. He is mindful to keep me apprised of the state of my finances, for better or worse. We'd been doing okay, helping each other out, but five seasons of disastrous fires had driven prices of fire insurance into the stratosphere. We were both on fixed incomes, so everything was already suffocatingly tight. That day he gave me the bad news: the perfect storm had hit. Both the fire insurance and property taxes were due, and the property taxes had gone up again. I was $1,000 short. He told me he'd prayed. A lot. What could we do? He thought maybe he'd get a job mastering someone's songs, or I'd help somebody write a book, or there would be lots of sales of our books on Amazon. It was all possible and had happened before, but those jobs would be like tiny drops in a big, empty bucket. At that point, the only thing we could do was pray (a lot) and wait.

"Your father knows you have such needs," Jesus said. "Consider the lilies of the field. Consider the birds of the air. Your Heavenly Father feeds them every day—all of them."

God is a good Father. Every good and perfect gift comes down from the Father of Lights Who is not arbitrary, capricious, erratic, unreliable, untrustworthy, inconsistent, or changeable. He says what He means, and He keeps His promises. He knows how to give good gifts to His children, and He knows what we need even before we ask. Jesus told us to pray to our Father in heaven, *"Give us this day our daily bread."* He will always provide for His children. And many times He has told me, *"I will never leave you, fail you, or forsake you."* Even in this current mountainous obstacle, somehow He would work all these things together for good. And He did, but the way He did it is so surprising that it would be impossible to believe except it happened right under my feet.

Dan was on his way down to the storage area under my house to empty the buckets that caught the drips from a leaking water filter he'd managed to fix many times, though somehow it would find a way to have another wayward leak somewhere else. Every day he had to check the buckets and empty them under the trees in the yard.

When he came back upstairs later that day, he told me he'd found a rat in one of the buckets. "The poor guy must have been in there for hours," he said. "He was totally spent, barely able to keep his nose above the water. I took the bucket outside and carefully poured him out on the ground. He lay there panting but not moving, so I picked him up, rubbed his back, and held him in the sunshine to warm him up." Then Dan put the rat in a shallow box with some paper towels and placed it back in the storage area.

Ever since my cat died, the storage area has become a haven for rats. Dan has done some humane trapping and releasing, but it hasn't significantly reduced the population down there. So I wasn't thrilled when he told me that he brought the rat back into the storage area.

"Why did you do that?" I demanded with some annoyance. "We're trying to get rid of them, and you've let him go so he can go make more babies to add to the colony under my house."

"I didn't want to leave him outside where other animals could get to him, and where he didn't know where he was," Dan explained. "I thought he'd have a better chance of surviving if he were back in a place he knew."

What could I say? Dan hates killing things. That's just who he is. I sighed and shook my head. But I didn't complain. There's something very sweet about his tenderhearted respect for life and the creatures God has created.

Dan told me, "Before I left the storage area, I went to pet the rat one more time. When I did, he leapt up and started trying to get out, so I tilted the box on its side and he staggered out like a drunk, fell on his side, then got up and walked a little farther between some storage boxes where he stopped and started to clean himself. That was a good sign, so I left him there."

The next day, Dan went back to see if the rat had recovered or if his body would need to be removed. I was working at my computer when Dan came rushing up the stairs, excitedly declaring, "The rat paid me for saving his life! I looked where I last saw him," he said. "He wasn't there—but something else was: two one-hundred-dollar bills folded together in half, one torn with a hole in it, and both of them chewed on the edges with little tooth marks."

He showed me the folded bills to prove he wasn't making it up. We were both amazed. What a surprising way to answer our prayers!

Immediately, I wrote it down. The symbolism couldn't have been more obvious: We too felt as if we had been struggling not to drown, barely keeping our noses above water and wondering how long we could keep from going under. Suddenly, there was this money. A miracle of God's provision. Where did it come from?

Dan had a feeling there was an envelope involved. He said a human must have put the money there and forgotten about it. He kept saying that my late husband, Dennis, must have put it there in storage. I said Dennis had never done anything like that, and he certainly wouldn't have had crisp, brand-new hundred-dollar bills that he could stash away somewhere. My mom liked to do that—get new $100 bills from the bank and put them in Kleenex boxes and between pages of magazines. She always told me to check everything in the house after she died because she liked to hide money but often forgot where she'd put it.

It was a mystery, but one too good not to share. Dan started texting his sisters, telling them about the rat that paid him for saving its life.

The next day, Dan went down to empty the buckets. I wondered if he'd find more money, but dismissed it as a silly thought. Nevertheless, when Dan came up the stairs, I quipped, "Did the rat leave you a tip?"

Dan said, "He didn't leave me another two one-hundred-dollar bills." He paused, looked at me, then blurted, "He left me eight!" I was incredulous, but Dan held them in front of my face—eight crisp, new one-hundred-dollar bills. And all of them had little teeth marks on the edges.

Dan said he had decided to check the spot again. "Not that I expected anything would be there," he grinned. "But there was. Very close to where the bills had been the day before were things that had the color of money. When I looked closer, I saw it was eight more one-hundred-dollar bills scattered in about a two-foot radius, and they were flat, not folded. Nearby was a brand-new strip of Liberty Bell Forever stamps."

We could hardly believe it. If I hadn't seen it for myself, touched the stamps, and run my fingers over the little tooth marks on the bills, I don't know that I could have swallowed such a story. And both days, all this was left right where Dan had let the rat go free.

"You can be sure I told everyone I knew," Dan said, "my family, my friends, and I took pictures of the edges of the bills where the tooth marks were."

At the same time, he was mystified. How did the money get there? Did God materialize it? Was the rat looking for something to build a nest and tried the bills? All had teeth marks on their edges. He must have dragged them out from somewhere. Perhaps he'd tried to chew the bills and found them unsuitable for comfortable nesting. But why the stamps? And why didn't they have any teeth marks at all?

Dan had been sending texts to his sisters, sharing his conjectures of possible scenarios. His sister Becky suggested he look at the dates on the bills. That was a very smart idea. Dates ranged from 1997 to 2006. He also checked the date on the stamps. They were issued in 2006.

That eliminated Dan's two main suspects. My mother died in 2004. In 2006, Dennis had multiple strokes, and my son John had taken him to live with him in Oregon.

Intrigued, Dan searched the storage area. He found a wicker basket with a hole chewed in the bottom and surmised that the rat could have found the money in the basket and pulled it out through the hole. He emptied the basket on the floor and looked through everything but decided the money hadn't come from there.

A couple of days later, Dan noticed a large paper gift bag about four feet to the left and a little farther back of where he'd found the money. Somehow he hadn't seen it before. Upon closer inspection, he saw there was a hole chewed in the bottom left corner.

He emptied the contents onto the floor and went through them pretty quickly. There were miscellaneous items such as a used buckwheat pillow, old magazines, and Auto Club travel guides. He flipped through the pages and shook them to see if anything fell out. There was a red plastic object he couldn't identify and other things too, but to him, they just looked like junk.

Since he had to get going, and thinking that nobody was likely to go down to that area soon, he left the items scattered on the floor and went off to empty the buckets. He figured the rats would leave everything alone because they tended to be wary of anything that had been recently moved.

The next day when he was on his way to empty the buckets, he noticed the red plastic object had been moved. So had a few other items from the bag. *Uh oh!* He thought. He didn't want the buckwheat pillow to be chewed and its contents scattered across the floor. So he gathered up the items and put them on his lap. Since he was not in a hurry that day, he decided to check each thing as he put it back into the bag.

When he lifted up one of the first items in the pile on his lap, he noticed a flash of something that was the color of money. There was a white envelope with a ragged hole that looked like something had taken a two-inch bite out of its bottom edge. And showing just below the deepest part of the bite was a hundred-dollar bill in pristine condition. There wasn't a single tooth mark on its clean, smooth edges.

Carefully, Dan examined the gift bag itself. On one side, in large letters printed in marking pen, it said "CARIE," the name my parents called me from the time I was a little girl. Excitedly, Dan brought the envelope up to show me and told me what he'd discovered. After that, we quickly pieced together the truth of the matter.

In January 2007, I turned sixty. My father drove up to celebrate with me in person and deliver my birthday present—a sleek, dark gray Dodge Magnum with a Hemi engine. Really? A Hemi? What sixty-year-old needs a muscle car with that much power? Daddy said it was a safety feature—for passing other vehicles. He sounded perfectly serious, but I think he was chuckling inside when he said it.

Daddy had packed the car with things from the house, many of which had been used in my mother's care. Since there was a lot, whatever he brought was taken to storage. Among those items was a gift bag he likely intended as part of my birthday blessing. I'm sure he put the envelope of cash in the bag for me to find later. He loved giving gifts—and making them surprises.

I cannot explain how I felt when the exact amount I needed for property taxes appeared in my storage area—plus an extra hundred dollars. Why that last bill remained in the envelope, untouched, is a mystery. I think God wanted us to find it to show us the source of the surprise my father intended for me, and to know that He, my Father God, had kept it there for seventeen years until the moment I needed it most. He revealed it in a way that was definitely a surprise.

When Dan showed me the first two hundred-dollar bills, I wished I could keep one—with those little tooth marks—to feel and remember this astonishing provision, and to show others as proof that it really happened. But when the other eight bills came, I knew I couldn't keep one because it took $1,000 to help pay the property taxes.

When the eleventh bill appeared, I knew it was a direct gift. I asked Dan to give me the one with the hole in it and the envelope with the big chewed opening. I propped it up where I could see it daily, a reminder that my all-wise, omniscient Father God knows my needs and how to meet them.

Now, rats in the basement are a nuisance, and so is a leaky water filter that doesn't seem to stay fixed. But God used both of these troubling things to provide the money for the bill I couldn't possibly pay.

Before Dan left to pay the property taxes, I prayed that no one would be in line, that God would choose who would be at the window, and that Dan would have the opportunity to tell the clerk how God had provided the money in such an unusual way. All of that happened. When Dan paid the taxes, no one was in line to be inconvenienced while he shared the story with the woman at the window, pointing out the tooth marks on the bills. He said she seemed to enjoy the account of the unlikely means of provision. He added that she didn't seem to be a Christian, so I prayed that she would be intrigued and desire to know this remarkable God for herself.

Other surprises were yet to come. God had more blessings to reveal to me. Inside the bag were items that were worthless and meaningless to anyone but me. The buckwheat pillow was the one Daddy and I had placed under Mom's head when she no longer had the strength to turn it herself. Daddy wanted me to have it. Seven years we cared for her together, and the worse things got, the closer we three became. My father became the daddy of my dreams.

Those tour books came from several road trips Daddy and I took across the country after Mom died. We retraced lands they had walked together and visited their longtime friends and Mom's beloved nieces and nephews.

My daddy loved providing for me—a house, a car, a baby grand—and now he wanted me to have memories, to see landscapes and places I could never visit on my own. He insisted we go to St. Petersburg to marvel at glorious architecture unlike anything else in the world. He loved to surprise me with experiences spectacular enough that I would remember them—and the one who had provided them—for the rest of my life.

But you know what touched me the most? The little strip of Forever stamps. When he was a boy, my daddy loved collecting stamps, and when I was little, he taught me to love them too. Even throughout all the years I was a married woman with a family of my own, he would send me plate blocks of the prettiest new stamps he could find. He must have loved the idea of the new kind of stamp that would always be worth whatever first-class postage was, no matter how high the cost had gone.

I've been thinking about this whole event—the leaks, the rat, the timely, miraculous provision in such an impossible way—but I can't help pondering the presence of the lone strip of Forever stamps near the money, the only other item included in the array. Why would my Heavenly Father tell the rat to extricate this small item from where it was sandwiched between books and magazines and instruct it to place it carefully where it couldn't be missed?

My daddy went to be with Jesus fourteen years ago, and I still dream about him often. Many times, we're going somewhere, or he's showing me how to take the safest way home. I miss him still. Somehow, that little strip of Forever stamps felt like having my daddy back—just for a moment. It said, "I love you and was thinking of you, even though you had grown up and live so many miles away."

This last expression of my daddy's desire to provide for me—revealed by my Heavenly Father in such an unusual, surprising, and spectacular way—is a gift of love from both givers—something to treasure and to remind me of them for the rest of my earthly life. Someday, I will be with them forever in the place prepared for me, where there are no leaks, no bills, no sorrow, no tears, no death, and no pain.

In the meantime, my Heavenly Father will continue to provide for me, guide me, and show me the safest way Home.

Meaningless Suffering

After interviewing survivors of the Holocaust, a rabbi concluded it's *meaningless* suffering that defeats us. It's all about knowing God's heart. Can you trust Him through unremitting horror and pain?

If He's God—if He's omniscient and powerful enough to stop evil, if He's just, good, and loving—how can He let this go on any longer? More than one follower of Jesus has turned away when a loved one died, deciding that God was either not there or didn't care. Even Jesus' hand-picked disciples were offended, stumbled, distrusted, and fell away when He didn't oust Rome and set up His Kingdom. Instead, He let Himself be led away, bound, to be mocked, scourged, beaten, and crucified. He didn't match their expectations of what He was supposed to be or do. So they ran away.

Of course, He had a far bigger plan—something better than stopping Roman rule. But it didn't look like it at the time. For a while, it was nothing but meaningless suffering—until the third day…

So maybe an answer to why God doesn't do things the way we think He should is that there's a bigger picture, with more at stake than we know, and it makes no sense to us because we don't have all the information or know everything He knows.

There was no meaningless suffering in my mother's illness, even though it became as awful as ALS. It was heart-rending, back-breaking (we had to turn her every two hours), but it healed our relationship, which had been difficult. She became the mom of my dreams.

I remember standing at the foot of her bed, saying my final goodbyes to the still form that had been my mom, when I heard God say, "The blessings will far exceed the suffering and sorrow." I said, "There was a lot of suffering and sorrow."

But in the twenty years since my mom went to heaven, there has been so much blessing, and it keeps on coming like a river that is always full of fresh, clear water.

One of the blessings came from a promise I made to my mom as she worried, "Who will take care of you when you're blind? Who will take care of you when I'm gone?"

I told her, "Don't worry, Mom. I'll get one of those cool dogs."

Without that promise and my increasing blindness, I never would have gotten a guide dog. Hedy gave me one of the most extraordinary relationships in my life. Plus, it opened whole worlds of communities I never could have otherwise entered or even known about.

I particularly love the volunteers who transform rambunctious, unruly puppies into confident, unflappable dogs who can be trusted to keep a blind person safe and give us an enviable life instead of one sighted people pity.

I tell you, those who take an eight-week-old puppy, give up sleep, unstained carpets, unchewed furniture, and peace and quiet for eighteen months while they work to give the young dog house manners, security, and adaptability to all sorts of environments, noises, smells, and circumstances—and then, when it's beautifully trained, give it back to the guide dog school—are a very special kind of human being.

Heather was fourteen when she took on her first puppy, a small black Lab named Hedy. I'm so grateful for what Heather and her family did in preparing that difficult puppy for service. She was hard-headed, self-willed, independent, but the family prayed for her, and they also prayed for a whole year for the blind person God would choose to be her partner.

At the same time, I was praying for a whole year for the dog that God would choose for me. And, unbeknownst to each other, we prayed for the successful forging of our partnership all through my twenty-eight days at guide dog school.

Good thing—because Hedy was a handful, and I worried the whole time I was being trained at the school that I would not be able to manage her and would be sent home dogless, in shame.

But they prayed, and I prayed, and Hedy and I graduated with honors, and she changed my life. We went places. We did things. I traveled more. I had more joy. She ended the isolation and devastation of catastrophic loss, and inspired six books, while providing many chances to talk to people about the good that can come even when you can no longer see.

A lot of suffering preceded those blessings. There are many things about being blind that I really don't like. I'm not telling you that God has made it a thing of beauty.

I remember one night standing out by my mailbox, looking up at the sky. It was black. Wistfully, I thought, *I wish I could see the stars.*

God said, "In heaven, you won't miss a thing."

Then He asked, "Will you do this for Me?"

Would I do what? Be blind?

"Yes. Be blind and trust Me to take you through it. Be blind and let Me turn it to good. Be blind and not resign yourself to increasing loss, but accept it as a source of opportunities you never would otherwise have."

It's been years since God and I had that conversation. I am much blinder than I was then, and some days are frustrating. I feel helpless and disabled, bereft of contrast and colors and the faces of people I love. I miss seeing the subtleties of paintings that used to thrill my heart. I miss being able to tell what I'm looking at or find the lid I just took off a jar.

But I trust Him. I trust Him to turn it to good.

Someday, I will see colors unlike anything in the visible spectrum on Earth. In the meantime, I feel Him walk beside me in a partnership richer than with Hedy, and every day I find Him faithful, trustworthy, and good.

I want to tell you one more story that would not have happened had I not been blind.

Among the dozens of puppy raisers I've met over the years is a young woman who became a friend. One day, she told me she was worried.

Ever since childhood, she had heard a voice telling her she had to kill someone before she was thirty. She was now twenty-nine, and her birthday was coming up soon.

So we prayed.

She's a wife now and a mom to an active, adorable little girl. We don't have time to talk anymore, but she emails every so often when she gets a chance.

Recently, she wrote, "I'm thirty-three now and still haven't killed anyone, not even myself."

This is the kind of wonderful interweaving of lives and love that has happened in my last forty-eight years of surprising adventures with Jesus. Many times, I have seen Him turn the worst into the best, and He tells me, "You ain't seen nothin' yet!"

Carie

"I think she's going to be a very calm dog and kind of quiet," Dan said, holding toward me the tiny black-and-white puppy he had just brought home from the animal shelter. I looked at her sweet little face. She sure was cute. And quiet.

"I'm going to call her Carie," he said.

Carie was quiet because she was sick. The next day, she was listless and didn't want to eat. She could barely walk, and then she started throwing up. Dan called the shelter and said,

"Something's wrong with this dog I got from you yesterday. She's really sick."

They told him the entire litter had come down with Parvo and had already been euthanized. They didn't want him to return Carie for fear of exposing the other dogs in the shelter, but they offered to send her to a specific clinic to have her put down. They also told him they wouldn't refund the $40 adoption fee he had paid.

"I didn't want to get her euthanized," he said, "but I also didn't want to pay a lot of money to try to do something about Parvo, which they usually die from anyway. So I looked at her and said, 'Well, you're either going to make it or you're not. And that's the way it goes.' I wasn't going to spend any money on her. I grew up where people weren't willing to spend thousands or even hundreds of dollars on their pets because they had to feed their families.

"I'd had that dog for one day. I wasn't connected to her. I had no relationship with her. I had no idea who she was."

Dan fixed Carie a bed in a cardboard box and put it on the front porch where she would be warm but not too hot. Then he left for the store.

When he returned, the box was empty.

He wondered, *Where could she be? She can't be far because she can barely move.*

"I went around the back of the house," he said. "I looked around the front, checked by the lemon trees, and went down by the lake. I searched all over the yard and garage and couldn't find her."

Dan lived near a lake at the bottom of a steep hill covered with tall, dry grasses and weeds. He stared at the hill's pale, monochrome sides. Surely it would be easy to spot a black-and-white dog there, no matter how small. But when he scanned the area, he didn't see her. He figured she couldn't have gone that far, weak as she was, but since she wasn't near the house, he decided to search the hill anyway.

The ground was uneven and treacherous, and the dry earth crumbled beneath his feet. He had been searching for about half an hour and was considering giving up when his foot slipped, and he found himself falling.

"I'd stepped on an old wine bottle that was hidden under the weeds," he said. "It rolled out from under my foot, and I fell forward onto my hands and knees. There, under the dry grass, between my right hand and my right knee, I saw a flash of black and white. I thought, *What's that?*

"I moved the grass, and there was Carie, curled up in a small hole."

Quickly, Dan cleared the grasses from the opening and lifted the tiny puppy out of the hole she had crept into to die. The little dog lay limp in his hands. She didn't look strong enough to make it even one more day.

Veterinarians are expensive. What should he do?

Dan said, "God spoke to me right then and said, 'You chose her. She's your responsibility. You take care of her.'" I thought, *Oh. Okay. That's that.*

"Now, I'm not used to having God speak to me like that. If I hear anything, I usually think it's me making it up. But as soon as I saw Carie in that hole, God hit me like a lightning bolt. It was very clear. I wasn't going to argue with Him about it.

"It was obvious. I mean, what are the chances I'd find this little puppy on a hillside, in a hole under the weeds, by tripping over a hidden bottle and falling right where she was? It's impossible. It's like a trillion to one that that's going to happen."

So Dan took Carie to the vet and told them she had Parvo. They said they'd see what they could do. Parvo is deadly for puppies, but God had spoken, so Dan knew he had to try. Regardless of the outcome, he had to try.

Every day, he made the half-hour drive to the vet to see Carie. He massaged her and talked to her, encouraging her to live. After ten days, she was well enough to go home with him.

Why is this one of my favorite stories?

God wanted Dan to find the puppy, and He worked a small miracle so he would—but Dan had to go looking for her. Then God spoke to him, another little miracle, and Dan chose to act upon it, investing in the helpless, unknown puppy, time-consuming and expensive as it was.

Carie grew up into a healthy, energetic dog who was anything but calm and quiet. But she brought a lot of joy to the people who knew her—even the cranky neighbor across the street from Dan's workplace who hated dogs. Something about her lively personality got past his grumpy ways and made him smile.

We are partners in God's purposes on Earth. It's not all about miraculous divine intervention, and it's not all about human effort. It's a combination of the two that brings about opportunities to give life to the helpless, the lost, the dying. Each life matters. God designed it that way. And He cares about each one, even little sick puppies. He knows what each life can become, and He is pleased to see what we choose to do to help Him bring it about.

The Intended End

Every account in this book comes from the mundane, ordinary, and unspectacular events in the daily lives of people I have known for a very long time. In each story is a glimpse of the heart of God, whose thoughts toward us—more than the grains of sand—are for good and not for evil, to give us a future and a hope.

Life can be hard, full of distress and loss, with circumstances that overwhelm us and sorrows that seem insurmountable. But we are not meant to go it alone, helpless bystanders watching in hopeless resignation. There are opportunities Jesus will open before us if we ask Him to show us what we cannot see with our physical eyes. There are things we have been designed to do—good works that the Lord of the Universe Himself prepared before the beginning of time. We are part of a vast tapestry that stretches beyond human history, yet within that unimaginable masterwork, each of us has something to do that will make a significant difference. It cannot come about by our most strenuous human efforts or our amazingly facile and brilliant brains; it requires supernatural divine guidance and Holy Spirit power. And we have it every day as we walk in harmony with the One who loves us most.

And now, at the end of this book, this is what He wants to say to you:

He wants you to know Him. He wants you to hear Him. He wants you to trust Him as you face each difficult thing. He is faithful. His timing is perfect. His name is I AM, and He is ever working on your behalf for your eternal good. He came to restore what was lost in the Garden—fellowship with our Creator, walking and talking together as Friend to friend, never again to be separated from His perfect love. It's what He intended all along.

All throughout this book, He has been calling to you, inviting you into His Great Adventure, and now He is saying to you:

"I found you when you were lost, lifted you out of the hole where you sat in darkness under the shadow of death, and paid a very high price so you might live. I didn't do it so you'd owe Me; I did it because I love you. Together, we have something to do as unique as you are. Your life matters to Me.

You are here to change what would be without you.

I chose you.

I AM responsible for you.

I will take care of you."

www.ingramcontent.com/pod-product-compliance
Lightning Source LLC
Chambersburg PA
CBHW071843020426

42331CB00007B/1841